CONFLICT
CHARACTER &
INFLUENCE

I0617851

CONFLICT
CHARACTER &
INFLUENCE

Pleasing God Through Building Effective Relationships

BRENT MAXWELL &
FRANKLIN SMITH

MEDIA.COM

CONFLICT
CHARACTER &
INFLUENCE

Copyright © 2022 by Franklin Smith and Brent Maxwell

The views and opinions expressed in this book are those of the author and do not necessarily reflect the official policy or position of Illumify Media Global.

Published by
Illumify Media Global
www.IllumifyMedia.com
"Let's bring your book to life!"

Paperback ISBN: 978-1-955043-18-2

Cover design by Debbie Lewis

Typeset by Art Innovations (http://artinnovations.in/)

Printed in the United States of America

This book is part of a program and community dedicated to effective discipleship and influence.

Please find us at:

- Website - 95FIVE.com
- Instagram - @95Five.Official
- Facebook - @95FiveBookOfficial
- YouTube - @95Five

DEDICATION

Each person on earth is faced with thousands of choices over the course of their life but just a single choice, good or bad, can dramatically change the health of their relationships. The decisions we make, especially when they impact others, become the source of our credibility and help define people's perception of us.

We dedicate this book to those who model good behavior and decision-making, and also to those who recognize where a course correction is necessary and trust God to guide them toward a resolution that pleases Him.

CONTENTS

Foreword   xi

Before You Read This Book   xv

Introduction: *What Would God Tell You about the Health
of Your Relationships with the People in Your Life?*   xix

1. Is There Evidence I Might Be Slightly Off Course
    in My Life and Relationships?   1
2. How Is Wisdom Manifested in How
    I Manage My Life and Relationships?   9
3. What Brings Out the Me that People See?   22
4. What Is My Go–to Strategy for Pressure?   33
5. What Is My Default Strategy for Managing Stress?   46
6. Do I See Evidence of Emotional Damage in Myself?   59
7. Are My Relational Stress Fractures Negatively
    Affecting Others?   71
8. What if I Could Manage My Relationships Differently?   84
9. How Do I Prepare to Strengthen My Relationships?   99
10. How Can I Strengthen My Relationships?   110
11. What Is Behind How I Manage My Pressure and
    Relationships?   125
12. How Am I Viewed by Others?   138
13. How Do I Ensure Integrity in My Beliefs?   151
14. Am I Ready to Build My Relationships?   160

Conclusion: *Based on What I Have Learned, Should
I Consider a More Effective Strategy?*   170

Where to Go from Here   172

About the Authors   177

FOREWORD

The first time I ever faced conflict was when I was three years old. My grandmother told me over the years how this event took place, but the details of the evening are vague. I remember waking up in bed and walking down the hallway of our home. I remember the floor was hardwood and my pajama feet would slip as I walked.

The small living room was filled with everyone in my family and extended family. My grandmother's cigarette smoke filled the air, and the chatter among my family was filled with tears and, yes, conflict. My mother and father, who were only in their early twenties, were making the decision to divorce, and by the time the smoke cleared from our living room, my life would change.

As my grandmother told the story, my mother was crying and saw me walking toward her. She brought me close to tell me that she and my father would no longer be living together. She then asked me who I would want to go with. I ran to my father, and that's when I started my life with a single father in his early twenties, and a mother who loved me, but with whom I slowly drifted apart as I found a new meaning of home.

This story, unfortunately, is all too common. I'm not unique. I must have paid good attention to the details, because thirty-five years later, I introduced my two beautiful daughters to the same conflict. I had developed a knack for managing around conflict, but not for managing the conflict itself. What happens when we manage around a challenge is that we develop habits that add to our pressure, develop stress, and damage the influence and character that humans are so dependent on in relationships. This happened to me, and the damage to my family was the consequence.

In 2017, I had enough. I was tired of trying to manage conflict without positive results. Instead, the measurable results came in the form of broken relationships, lost trust, and personal ruin. So, what changed that made me want to redefine how people perceived me and judged my character? When I looked in the rear–view mirror of my life, I saw carnage that directly impacted the people I loved and cared for most. Something had to change, and everything in me told me that change had to start with me.

The problem with wanting to change when you are in the midst of extreme pressure is that you are often too busy managing brokenness in every part of your life. Even those who appear to have it all together will face unique challenges when the decision to change the fabric of their character is made. I knew that if I were to sincerely address issues in my life, I would need an advocate to learn with.

I reached out to my close friend, Brent Maxwell, who I love deeply and who I trust. This trust was not built on his willingness to appease my pride and affirm me but was founded on hours of conversation between the two of us over multiple years where we both decided to dive into our conflicts, relationships, and the collateral damage that was caused. Brent had spent over thirty years as a pastor, but even after all these years of talking to hurting souls, he was experiencing his own conflicts that he no longer wanted to manage around.

We decided there is power in community, and we determined to start by creating a community of two.

We did not know where to start, but with Brent's extensive knowledge of the Bible, we decided to explore what God had to say on the subject. Three years later, we believe we have assembled an organized way to present this content, and we hope you will find value in these pages.

I have seen tremendous change in my life since then, but that does not mean I no longer deal with conflict or the challenges that come from previous conflict. I will say, however, that now I have a strategy to manage the conflict as opposed to managing around the challenge. More importantly, I'm learning to attack how potential conflict will impact those affected by my life so that I can minimize collateral damage.

This is the type of person I want to be. Does this mean I have redemption with all who have been affected by my choices? No. I do, however, have clarity in how I will work toward restoration in my character, and that my choices moving forward will prove I am accountable, and I am growing. That's what I have control over.

People are worth the effort, even if it took me so long to open my eyes to that fact. Now, with God's direction and a growing community of believers, Brent and I can build a foundation for our character that holds up under the storms that life brings. This is not a story about my testimony. This is a testimony of how God's word changes people from the inside out when we take the time to seek His timeless and powerful message and apply that wisdom into being a new creation in Christ.

BEFORE YOU READ THIS BOOK

The book you are about to read is part of a larger picture. It is an introduction to our relationship principles, which we believe has great potential to get you centered again on the most critical part of the mission God has for you on earth: To accomplish His will by providing a godly influence in the lives of those who are in your personal world.

Godly influence in our relationships, we believe, is the most important missionary activity there is.

We take Jesus' approach to ministry and teaching as our example. He spent His entire ministry in His home country, and most of that in the northern parts where He was from. He affected thousands of "strangers" by His teaching and miracles, but His urgent mission was to prepare the small group of people who followed Him and embraced His message.

Of that group of followers and supporters there were twelve who would become His apostles. One of them betrayed Jesus and destroyed himself. He was replaced later by another. Among the eleven who remained faithful, three were set apart further as His closest confidants. Of those three, one was His best friend.

The point is, Jesus was very much relational, a human image of the character of the Heavenly Father. Within the strategic and mathematical mind of God He understood the power of multiplication. He didn't spend His energy on vast additions to His mission but on a few who, through the wonders of multiplication, would bring true additions later.

Effective churches and missionaries understand the abundance that comes from multiplication. It is why Christianity has spread around the world and has endured for two-thousand years. God's power working through His people utilizing His strategy of multiplication gives His message its continued presence in an otherwise dark world.

Human nature being what it is, however, is prone to the distraction of preferred outcomes, even in our evangelism.

We labor under expectations from our own standards or the standards of others, particularly those we perceive from a competitive spirit, and design methodology and experience that circumvents the patterns shown us in Scripture. We attempt mass addition rather than strategic multiplication. We must keep our focus on that strategy.

Churches that very wisely emphasize small groups, or believers who belong to them, engage in the disciple-making strategy taught by Christ. A challenge that arises in that environment, however, is navigating logical parameters we assign to our groups (age, gender, parents, singles, etc.). There is natural affinity in these categories, obviously, but it could be that further relatability can be found in relationships within those groups.

Within small groups are micro groups of individuals learning and living effective relationship skills that are mutually beneficial.

The hundred or so individuals who followed or supported Jesus was his "congregation", so to speak. The twelve disciples set apart from them and destined to be apostles were His small group. He spent most of His time on that level.

Going deeper we find three, Peter, James, and John, the micro group who would fill particularly significant roles in the new church after Jesus ascended back to His Father. Peter would help shepherd the Jewish church into existence and beyond the boundaries of ethnic Israel into the Gentile world. James would be one of the first martyrs. John, Jesus' best friend, would endure until old age and pen the great apocalyptic visions of the end of the age when Jesus will return and set Creation right once again.

The effectiveness of small and micro groups have not changed. 95FIVE has invented nothing, but we would like to help turn our focus back to the strategy Christ established.

In presenting this book to you, we are asking you to consider being a part of the effort to strategically extend your church's ministry with the power of micro groups.

In the meantime, please read the following chapters carefully and prayerfully to learn the foundation of God's relationship skills with which you can please Him by being effective, influential, and authentic to those He entrusted to you. We will describe our definition of micro groups at the end of this book, as well as the program that comes with your purchase.

You can also find more information about 95FIVE and our approach to relationships in the context of church micro groups at **95FIVE.com**.

INTRODUCTION:
WHAT WOULD GOD TELL YOU ABOUT THE HEALTH OF YOUR RELATIONSHIPS WITH THE PEOPLE IN YOUR LIFE?

There is something we long for: the ability to wake up each morning without worry or concern. After all, mornings like that are a preview of God's design for each day when we enjoy the prospect of fresh opportunities to do good without the weight of negative pressure to distract us. We don't want a life free of challenges, just a way to manage those challenges with hope and optimism rather than anxiety and intimidation.

God made us in His image with the ability to make choices and to be relational. Those two gifts, when used in conjunction with His principles and direction, create mornings of peace and worry–free relationships. If you are like most humans on this earth, however, many of your days are filled with managing the consequences of both your own choices and those of other people in your life.

Because God created us to be relational, He also gave us a road map to manage our relationships in a way that is pleasing to Him. As Christians, it is our desire to please God, but because we live in a fallen world, it is not always easy to do so. Therefore, we must be intentional in our pursuit to understand that road map if we are to please Him. It is an effort that will last a lifetime, and each relationship you are blessed with will have its own unique challenges and dynamics.

The Bible tells us, "But the wisdom from above is first pure, then peaceable, gentle, reasonable, full of mercy and good fruits, unwavering, without hypocrisy. And the seed whose fruit is righteousness is sown in peace by those who make peace" (James 3:17–18).

You are a good person who wants to create and enjoy peace. You always try to do your best and feel bad when you mess up. You love your family and friends. You are faithful to your spiritual beliefs and highly regard your place of worship. For the most part you are happy and content with the blessings God gave you. Many who know you value you as a part of their lives. It is certain you will be memorialized with plenty of love and words of affection when your time here is over.

However, like everyone else you have your share of challenges and anxieties. It is a part of life; this fallen world is no easy place. We all get pushed and pulled by forces we did not cause and decisions of others we cannot undo. Add to this any pain you do bring on yourself and you have ingredients that work against your happiness and sense of peace.

Again, that is all of us. We aren't perfect. We face the fruits of human weakness all the time. Even during those days when we feel we are doing everything right, we are vulnerable to the barbs of relational pain. When we experience them, a little bit more peace in our lives fades away for a while.

The Bible acknowledges this reality many times. Look at one of the examples in Psalm 37. Let's begin at verse one. King David, who knew a thing or two about the ups and downs of living in this world, began his psalm by saying: "Do not fret because of evildoers, be not envious toward wrongdoers. For they will wither quickly like the grass and fade like the green herb" (verses 1–2).

In his beginning words, David recognized a life pressure, the individuals who act wickedly and negatively affect others with their choices. These people aren't the only form of pressure that acts against us, but they exist. More common than them are all the good people in our lives who sometimes make decisions that add difficulty to our pursuit of happiness, just as we sometimes affect them in similar ways with our ineffective choices.

David continues. "Trust in the LORD and do good; dwell in the land and cultivate faithfulness" (verse 3). How are we to manage the challenges that come from the behavior of others? Instead of being consumed by resistance to what we cannot control, we shift our perspective toward goodness and God's faithfulness. It is easy to acknowledge God's faithfulness, but to purposefully view your life circumstances accordingly and to base your behavior to align with His goodness and faithfulness is quite another.

We need a change in our mindset. "Delight yourself in the LORD; and He will give you the desires of your heart" (verse 4). The word *desire* in this verse is often mistaken for all the things we want. However, it actually means *requests* or *petitions*.

Our hearts don't always value what God sees as important, but when we learn to find true joy in Him, our requests become more ordered to what reflects His will.

An effective mindset will lead to a corresponding approach to what and who is in your life. "Commit your way to the LORD, trust in Him, and He will do it" (verse 5). In the Hebrew language of the Old Testament, David is literally saying, "Roll your way, or path, onto God." This strategy invites God's wisdom to be our guidance in how we manage our challenges, particularly those caused by others.

The fruits of such an approach to God and life are the blessings of the validation of our faith. With the phrase "He will do it" is an assurance that your very creator will work toward the best possible outcome in your situation. Additionally: "He will bring forth your righteousness as the light and your judgment as the noonday" (verse 6). The clarity and wisdom of your trust in God will be revealed in a manner represented by the brightest sunlight of the day.

This is how Scripture teaches us. The Bible invites us to live in all the hope and optimism that God provides. This hopeful experience will not come to us because we are wishful, however. It comes because we choose to be strategic in our approach to life and relationships. Wisdom from Scripture prescribes a strategic, rather than passive, approach to survival and happiness.

Psalm 37 also shows us the opposite approach and consequence to strategy. "Do not fret because of him who prospers in his way, because of the man who carries out wicked schemes. Cease from anger and forsake wrath; do not fret; it leads only to evildoing" (verses 7–8). To fret means to burn with anger in the sense it is used in this portion of Scripture. We view it more as anxiety in our modern times, and that is an ineffective approach as well, one that could lead us to thought and behavior that would bring unpleasant consequences and further diminish our joy.

We have a source of wisdom that seeks to teach us the fine points of how we can best negotiate our way in this world. All we need to do is pray for wisdom and make simple adjustments to our perspective and approach to how we manage our challenges. That is what this book is about. We seek to accomplish three things:

FIRST, WE WANT TO LOOK WITH YOU INTO SOME OF THE MECHANICS OF OUR FAITH.

We learn a lot about *what* the Bible says about life and behavior, but often we neglect the *why* of those critical matters. God has reasons why He teaches us what He does. Understanding that will elevate your spiritual experience significantly. We will examine how we think as humans and the ways in which God wants to change our thought process to better reflect

His principles.

SECOND, WE WILL SHOW YOU SOME SIMPLE SHIFTS YOU CAN MAKE IN YOUR THINKING PROCESS TO PRODUCE A MORE EFFECTIVE APPROACH TO YOUR LIFE.

We refer to these shifts as simple adjustments, but that doesn't mean they are easy to make. They are not that difficult, either. It just takes the correct mindset. If you want more desirable results from how you approach life, these shifts are important to make in your life strategy.

FINALLY, WE WILL SHOW THE REAL FIELD OF OPPORTUNITY WHERE YOU CAN PLEASE GOD AND ACCOMPLISH HIS WILL.

We talk a lot in Christian circles about the need for missions and outreach to people groups in our own communities and around the globe. We should emphasize those opportunities to build God's kingdom and honor Christ's great commission (Matthew 28:18–20).

Missions are critical to the Christian community, but what about these other "commissions" from Jesus:

"Above all, keep fervent in your love for one another, because love covers a multitude of sins" (1 Peter 4:8).

"A new commandment I give to you, that you love one another, even as I have loved you, that you also love one another. By this all men will know that you are My disciples, if you have love for one another" (John 13:34–35).

Or, how about this one?

"Greater love has no one than this, that one lay down his life for his friends" (John 15:13).

No amount of cultural influence or religious commitment can compensate for a lack of attention to our personal relationships and the people God entrusted to us. If the Christian community does not emphasize that kind of ministry, we risk losing a lot of His anointing in everything else we do.

Relationships are everything, and we will give you some insight, based on many years of personal experience, into how you can adjust your thoughts to succeed in the most important ministry you have. If you are interested in preventing, or alleviating, needless emotional pain in your life and instead have an opportunity to really glorify the one who saved you, the information in the coming pages might be for you.

95FIVE is your aid in the pursuit of God's design for healthy relationships. Like you, we have experienced the devastation of how simple choices can create complex difficulties in the relationships we are trusted with. When choices outside of God's design compound the pressure and stress that negatively affect the health of our relationships, we feel diminished peace and ultimately a lack of harmony with God.

Our response to this pressure needs to be intentional in accomplishing two critical goals:

- To please God with the choices we make
- To please God in how we manage our relationships

This task isn't easy, but we can be encouraged because God never asks something of us without showing us how to accomplish it. His grace and comfort can be found in the lessons of His word that are available to us all. 95FIVE only exists to help connect you with those lessons with a fresh perspective. We hope you will link arms with us as we, the church community, pursue the joy of pleasing God with both our choices and relationships.

In the first chapter, we will share with you a personal experience of one of our team leaders and the lessons we took from it to create the foundation of what we teach. You will learn about the origin of 95FIVE.

IS THERE EVIDENCE
I MIGHT BE SLIGHTLY OFF COURSE
IN MY LIFE AND RELATIONSHIPS?

The Story of 95FIVE

Trust in the Lord with all your heart and do not lean on your own understanding. In all your ways acknowledge Him, and He will make your paths straight. (Proverbs 3:5–6)

The foundation of the 95FIVE approach to assessing our life and relationships comes from an experience of one of our founders. Here is Frank's story:

In November 1990, I was invited by a friend to explore a region of Mount St. Helens that had shown signs of recovery from the catastrophe it experienced ten years earlier when its volcano erupted and devastated the region. New growth was showing, and my friend was anxious to see if there were blacktail deer or the elusive Roosevelt elk repopulating the area.

We arrived at our launching spot on the designated morning before daybreak and with snowflakes swirling in the freezing air. My friend handed me a light pack with enough food and water for the day. I didn't bother checking the rest of the contents, as I should have done, thinking that with such an early start equipment like flashlights and extra clothing would not be an issue. We would be back before nightfall.

We split up but stayed in the same vicinity. He followed an old logging road, and I was sent up another way to check out the terrain. I studied a topography map the day before, so even though the territory was new to me I had an idea of what I would encounter.

The rising sun barely lit the way before me as I started out, but when I crested my targeted ridge at midday, I was stunned at the beautiful view. I explored a while and ate my lunch, then I checked my compass and map to determine my descent. We had agreed to meet at 4:00 that afternoon, well before dark.

I kept a lookout for the creek that would take me down to the road where we would meet. The farther down I traveled, however, the denser the foliage became until I was literally pushing my way through the brush.

I finally arrived at the creek, but nothing looked familiar. I was at a bend in the creek and noticed a very large tree that had survived the eruption and flooding. I continued to study my map and compass but was concerned I had made an error in my navigation.

My friend had lent me the day pack I was carrying because I did not have mine with me, so I sat down to review what resources were available to me. It was soon clear that we had different expectations for how to properly prepare for a day hike. There were no matches, lighter, fire–starting aids, and, of course, no flashlight. Because this incident took place before the age of cell phones and handheld GPS devices, I was at the mercy of the mountain.

Before the sun completely set, I managed to mark the large tree with some pink logging tape I found that morning. My strategy was to use the tree as a reference point as I set out to follow the creek to the truck. The problem was that I didn't know which direction to go.

The sun was now gone and the sky was cloudy, so there was no light from the moon or navigational help from the stars. Therefore, I decided to set out walking up-creek, having the sound of the moving water at my side as my only navigational aid.

For the next three hours, I stumbled through the darkness as shame set in with each step, because I knew better than to hike in unfamiliar wilderness without being properly equipped. After the fourth hour had passed, when I was near frozen, I sat down on a log to gather my thoughts. I assumed I went the wrong way and was even farther away from my friend than when I started.

As I sat there in silence considering my options, I heard something that got my attention. When I determined it was not a natural noise but a truck's horn, I realized that I had inadvertently hiked in the right direction, and after pushing my way through heavy brush, I found my friend waiting there for me. I can't describe the relief we both had.

The next day I received a call from my friend. He told me that he had done some checking around and learned that multiple people get lost in that exact area each year. Evidently, geologists had identified a large deposit of iron ore in that area, and it affected the magnetic needles of compasses.

I was shocked to hear this information and a bit relieved. I assumed I had made an error using my compass and that added to the embarrassment of getting lost. My friend asked me if I would be willing to come back to the mountain in a few days and do another hike.

I was hesitant, naturally, but he explained that what he wanted to do was see if we could find the point where I had begun my descent. If we did, then we could take careful measurements and hope that we would emerge at the giant tree with the pink tape. We would then continue to take measurements as we made our way back to the truck. The intention was to build a map that would benefit hikers by considering how far the compass could be off during their hikes. We agreed to give it a try.

A couple of days later we did as we planned, and my friend took great care in how he measured the distances between the descent starting point, the tree with the logging tape, and the truck. After calculating the measurements, he determined that over the five miles on the descent, the compass was off by about five degrees because of the iron ore deposits.

Five degrees was all it took to throw me off course enough to potentially end my life. To this day that fact remains heavily embedded in my memories. Five degrees off was enough to undo all that I had done right that day with my navigational skills. Another lesson I learned was that those five degrees would not have been quite as dangerous to me had I been better prepared for the unexpected.

FRANK'S EXPERIENCE TEACHES TWO VERY IMPORTANT LESSONS:

1. Negligence of just a few details can potentially cost you a lot later on.
2. You can be just five degrees off course in your life and relationships and find yourself lost in your attempts at managing them without direction.

Frank's insufficient pack provided lunch to eat, but nothing to help him through the eventual darkness and early winter cold in the mountains. He had navigational skills and plenty of experience, but even 95 percent effectiveness wasn't enough to overcome the perils caused by an invisible reality that created a false reading on his compass.

More than that, the invisible reality of the hidden iron ore deposits affected the guidance of an otherwise reliable navigational device, so much so that it got Frank considerably off course, enough to endanger his life.

Five percent ineffectiveness might not sound like much, and often it amounts to little in many circumstances. A 95 percent effective infielder would make a pretty good baseball player, but that 5 percent ineffectiveness could lose a game if the circumstances required 100 percent accuracy. If you elevate what is at stake, five percent is much more critical to an airline pilot or a surgeon.

We created the *95FIVE Relationship Program* because we acknowledge that potential chaos and pain can come from small percentages of neglect, unwise life choices, or even unawareness.

We also understand that there are a lot of unseen factors in life that can alter our course, even just a little bit. However, that slight change can have big differences down the road. If you walk across a field, five degrees won't make much difference in your destination. But if you are traveling miles? The difference is significant.

Ninety-five percent, five percent, and five degrees are symbolic numbers, obviously. Our point, however, is that it doesn't take much to damage our lives and relationships when life's pressures influence us to drift off course, often without our realizing it. How much pain do we experience because of choices such as:

- Making one or more unwise major purchases that we cannot really afford
- Lifestyle behaviors that seem inconsequential but after some time negatively affect our health
- Failing to address issues in a friendship that is vulnerable to failure
- Becoming insensitive to the needs of our spouse and children

We established 95FIVE to represent both the dangers and the possibilities in small percentages or in just a few degrees of our trajectory. A good deal of pain and chaos can come about from just a little neglect or inefficiency, but a lot of healing and joy come from just a small percentage of appropriate adjustment to our approach. In the same way, a few degrees off can cause us to miss our target by a great deal, but a few degrees of course adjustment can go a long way to getting us where we want to be.

No one is 100 percent effective all the time, but with strategy that is the application of wisdom, not only can we increase our percentages of effectiveness when required, but we can also potentially lessen the impact of being five degrees off due to the surprises that life springs on us. If you happen to be suffering from the consequences of being five degrees off course in your life, or of your own 5 percent ineffectiveness, there is still hope. Consider Frank's experience:

1. **He had his experience and maturity in the world of the outdoors to draw upon.** He had the sense to mark a tree for a reference point, and he knew to follow the sound of the creek as his guide through the darkness. Most of all, he didn't panic. That would have made the situation much worse.

2. **Someone else was involved in the situation.** Frank benefited from the fact that his friend was waiting by the truck, wondering what had happened. He kept honking the horn to give Frank a signal of where to go. That one thing saved the situation from getting much worse. Had he not heard the sound, an emergency crew would have been called out to look for him.

3. **God cared about him in those frightening moments.** If you think that statement is only a cliché, you don't understand the importance of God's love and providence in our trying situations. We believe God was very much involved in Frank's rescue.

Don't underestimate the insight you already have, or your capability to create a wise strategy. Some individuals may need specialized guidance before being ready for the 95FIVE approach to life and relationships, but chances are good you have plenty of understanding from experience to transform into wise strategy.

Also, don't underestimate the people in your life that will help. Some already are, whether you realize it or not. Others stand ready to partner with you in negotiating the challenges you are facing, whether they are family members, friends, or professionals.

Finally, give God the recognition He deserves for how He works in your life. Look for evidence of how He has been guiding and assisting you all along. As for wisdom? "But if any of you lacks wisdom, let him ask of

God, who gives to all generously and without reproach, and it will be given to him" (James 1:5). We urge you, however, to follow James's counsel that follows: "But he must ask in faith without any doubting" (James 1:6).

The first question to ask yourself, then, is: *Is there evidence that I might be slightly off course in my life and relationships?* The best evidence is damage in your relationships, no matter how insignificant it may seem to you. What you see might be drastically different from what someone else feels. Look for troubled spots in relationships. Examine other factors in your life as well, but relationships are the tell–tale sign of that 5 percent issue you may be reluctant to face.

Relationship damage is rarely the result of intentions. Often, it is a matter of small amounts of ineffectiveness. If being effective in relationships is important to you, and you want your intentions to be consistent with your results, it could be time for you to consider the power of strategy as your way of building, managing, and strengthening your relationships.

In the next chapter, we will discuss how wisdom and strategy is manifested in our relationships.

2

HOW IS WISDOM MANIFESTED IN HOW I MANAGE MY LIFE AND RELATIONSHIPS?

The Power of Wisdom in Your Connections to Others

The generous man will be prosperous,
and he who waters will himself be watered.
(Proverbs 11:25)

In this chapter, you will learn how to make a critical shift in your thinking and behavior to make your approach to your life and relationships richer and much more effective. You will discover:

- How you can understand your belief system
- An important change in your perspective that can make a big difference in how effective you are in life
- The formula that helps you find joy in the management of your life and relationships
- How to honestly and productively examine your behavior so that authentic positive change happens in how you live

Now that you have asked yourself if there is evidence that you are slightly off course in your life and relationships, it is time to address your answer to that question. Honestly, if you do not see any evidence of being five degrees off in some part of your life or at least one relationship, then you probably aren't reading this far. Since you are here, though, let's go a step further. Consider asking yourself another question: *How is wisdom being manifested in the way I manage my life and relationships?*

Admittedly, this can be difficult to answer. How do we know for sure if wisdom is expressed in how we live our lives and manage our relationships? To help with this, we would like to suggest asking a few more precise questions. A look at the parts of wisdom again will help us formulate these questions. Remember, wisdom is composed of

- Beliefs: your inner road map of reality
- Mindset: your attitude and outlook regarding your life and responsibilities
- Behavior: the outward expression of your beliefs and mindset through your actions and choices

When you learn to ask appropriate questions regarding these parts, you will learn the first of several critical shifts in your thinking and behavior that will vastly improve your life.

Let's begin by asking a question based on beliefs. We will examine beliefs in more detail in a later chapter, but for our purposes here, we can categorize them into higher beliefs and operational beliefs. What is the difference?

HIGHER BELIEFS

Your higher beliefs are ones regarding how you view reality. They include:

- Your religious beliefs
- Your views about the universe and nature

- Your overall philosophy about how everything should work
- Your moral and political opinions

OPERATIONAL BELIEFS

Your operational beliefs essentially make up the software that determines your decisions and behavior. Some examples are:

- What motives define how you spend your money
- What you do if someone spreads rumors about you
- How much your attitude changes if someone pushes in front of you at the grocery store
- Whether you yell or speak calmly when your children aggravate you

Most of us have the notion that our higher beliefs dictate our operational beliefs. We chalk up any deviation from our higher beliefs to momentary weakness, mistakes, or episodes of rebellion. There is more to it, though. The information we take in from our environment and experiences throughout the years plays a huge role in the formation of our operational beliefs.

Operational beliefs are concerned with survival, or more particularly, what brings pleasure and what avoids pain. With this categorization of your beliefs, you might ask, *Are my higher beliefs and my operational beliefs in alignment?*

Is it possible for them not to be? Would an authentic person of faith not adopt corresponding operational beliefs in their journey in life? Of course, but the key word is *adopt*. Whether we realize it or not, often we retain many misaligned operational beliefs, even after a meaningful spiritual conversion.

Look at an extreme example from the Bible. Judas, one of Jesus' disciples, was with Him for as long as the other disciples. He saw the same miracles and heard the same teaching. He may have actually believed Jesus was the Messiah. Otherwise, why stick around so long in a movement that might cost him his life?

In the end, though, what did he do? He betrayed Jesus. Why? Because his higher beliefs in God and at least the possibility of Jesus as the Messiah could not overcome his sense of security in money, which was one of his primary operational beliefs. Before he betrayed Jesus, we are told in Scripture that Judas was a thief (John 12:6). He stole from the disciples' shared funds. After he betrayed Jesus, he killed himself out of remorse. The lack of alignment in his belief system led to his tragic death as a spiritually lost soul.

A less extreme example, and one more relatable to us, was Peter, another of Jesus' disciples. He bragged about the fact that he would stick by Jesus' side even unto death, yet he was the one who denied knowing Him three times. Peter's higher beliefs were in God, in Jesus as the Messiah, and in the lofty ideals of bravery and loyalty. But he still had the operational beliefs of self-preservation at all costs. Therefore, he detached himself from his beloved rabbi's mission when he was identified as an accomplice.

He had great remorse as well. Fortunately, after His resurrection, Jesus restored Peter and made him much stronger as the future leader he would become. Unfortunately, however, he had a relapse when strict Jewish Christians came to visit the Gentile church in Antioch where Peter was staying for a while.

Paul, Peter, Barnabas, and other leaders were eating in fellowship with Gentile Christians, a religious taboo in the old Jewish world and still held on to by some of the Jewish Christians in the new faith. When these Jewish representatives of the Jerusalem church came up to visit the Gentile church in Antioch, Peter became intimidated and withdrew from the Gentile believers (Galatians 2:11–14). Self-preservation trumped his higher beliefs in the equality of all Christians, Jew and Gentile alike.

The guy who brought the gospel message to the Gentile world (Acts 10) now abandoned them to preserve his position and reputation in the church. Aligning our operational beliefs with our higher beliefs is a lifelong responsibility. Sometimes it is a joy to do so. Other times, it is a struggle. The more our beliefs align, however, the more effective we will be in life and relationships.

Think about ways you might struggle with this issue of misalignment in your belief system. Maybe your experience is similar to:

- Someone who insists on God's love and grace, yet who endures self-condemnation every time they make a mistake or fail
- A Christian who celebrates being made guiltless by the mercies of Christ but still uses guilt to discipline their children
- A person who believes in the importance of honesty but exaggerates their expense reports for business travel
- The church member who routinely replaces gossip with "prayer concerns"

Now, let's ask another question, this one regarding mindset: *What is my overall attitude in my approach to my life responsibilities and relationships?* In other words, what is your mindset regarding your stewardship of what God has entrusted to you, including your relationships? Especially your relationships!

We can define the mindsets regarding our life and relationship management in three types:

1. *I have to:* I am required by inflexible rules to manage my life a certain way
2. *I ought to:* A strong sense of obligation motivates my approach to living
3. *I get to:* I gladly address my responsibilities and relationships with a mindset that embraces opportunity

There are things we have to do: pay taxes and bills, mow our grass, do what our bosses tell us to do, etc. What we don't have to do, we should do. They are our many obligations.

We are obligated or strongly encouraged to behave in certain ways, but actually, no one is forcing us. In those cases, we view these matters as *I ought to*:

- I ought to pay more attention to my kids
- I should go to church regularly
- The right thing to do is stay at work a little after my shift is over if needed to make sure everything is in order before I go home

Then there are the *I get to* issues. They usually involve the activities we enjoy doing.

- I get to go shopping.
- I get to play golf this weekend.
- I get to eat ice cream.

It is almost as if we engage in these activities only when life gives us permission to do so, or we do them anyway, despite the nagging sense of obligation that we should be doing stuff we don't want to do.

Society and many of our own religious traditions have conditioned us to take a misguided view of what is required of us in life. That is not to say we can ignore our responsibilities and obligations and instead pursue only what pleases us. Of course not. But we can choose a mindset that keeps us anchored to principles and behaviors that make our lives more effective and enjoyable.

In our approach to life and relationships, everyone falls into one of the three above mindsets.

You will tend to view life according to whether you feel you have to, ought to, or get to.

You will have your own variation, but one of the general approaches will guide you. Which mindset you have is expressed in your attitude and behavior.

Have to people do what is required and hope that their faithfulness to what they believe is right alleviates their pain, punishment, or chaos most of the time. They don't get traffic tickets and are never accused of inconsistent church attendance. As for their relationships, they do their duty, however it is defined in a given relationship. Lack of trouble or chaos is their benchmark that determines whether their relationship is going well. *Have to* individuals are great people but they are vulnerable to resentment, disappointment, and legalism.

Ought to individuals feel the pressure of a life full of obligations. No one forces them to do these tasks, per se, but they know they should do them and often will. They wish to do what is right. Their vulnerability lies in missing out on the liberty and joy that comes with meeting their obligations. They stay faithful in their marriage because it is the right thing to do. They do a good job at work, go to their children's ball games, and volunteer at church because they know they should and such behavior yields favorable outcomes. However, they often grow weary from all the pressures of duty to their obligations, even service to God. They may not be unhappy, but that doesn't mean they have joy, either.

The *get to* mindset offers much greater effectiveness and emotional well-being. It avoids the insecurity of the *have to* mindset and burnout that often comes with the *ought to* approach. If you transfer your attitude to a *get to* orientation, you will experience a powerful shift in perspective and effectiveness. *Get to* people have more joy because they have learned to appreciate life's gifts and opportunities for growth.

Having a *get to* mindset might sound like a psychological gimmick, and there sure are many of those. However, there is a powerful experience from making an authentic shift from *have to* and *ought to* to *get to*. This is where wisdom comes into the picture.

We have found that if someone wants an authentic *get to* mindset shift, they will have a better chance if they embrace three important skills:

- Optimism: I have the liberty to choose to have a positive and hopeful mindset
- Gratitude: I am thankful for the chance to live life and experience its lessons and blessings
- Aspiration: I seek the best possible outcome in every situation

OPTIMISM

Optimism is an important part of the Christian outlook, yet it isn't employed in some Christian lives as it should be. We are optimistic about the afterlife, or about Jesus' victory over sin and death, but what about being optimistic that the wounds to your church fellowship will heal? How about the restoration of your rebellious teenager, or the cancer treatment of your friend?

Many people point out that optimism must be tempered with realism, but that suggests optimism isn't always realistic. We at 95FIVE believe it is, if it is genuine optimism. Yes, we live in a very imperfect world, but why not choose optimism over fatalism or pessimism? Not everything will work out according to our preferred outcomes, but a person with insight will understand that both positive and negative results have in their aftermath potential opportunities.

A person of faith will view all things as within the hand and purposes of God. Optimism is powerful. The lack of it is insulting to the providence of the Lord.

GRATITUDE

Gratitude is another underappreciated mindset. We all have heard lessons about being thankful. However, we still worry. We still grumble. We question God.

It really is difficult, if not impossible, to be thankful and bitter at the same time. If your prayers go along the lines of, "Lord, I'm thankful, but . . ." then it is possible that you are trying to be grateful, but you also reveal dissatisfaction. The apostle Paul said something important in this familiar verse: "Let the peace of Christ rule in your hearts, to which indeed you were called in one body; and be thankful" (Colossians 3:15).

ASPIRATION

The third component of a *get to* mindset is aspiration. Aspiration doesn't mean seeking out only what gets you what you want. It is more than setting personal life goals. It means having a perspective that motivates you to add value to others and make the best possible outcome of a given situation more likely.

Value that you add to other lives comes from actions such as:

- Providing counsel
- Helping someone through a crisis
- Modeling effective behavior
- Going above and beyond to make the company you work for more productive

There are countless ways you can add value to others' lives.

Aspiration adds value to other people's lives, and it purposely looks for better potential outcomes. Aspirational individuals are people you want to know. It is who you should want to be. You can only be that way if you are an optimistic and grateful person. You can be pessimistic and still bring some value to the life of someone else, but it won't be consistent or very productive. You will probably add a burden to someone rather than value.

Remember this formula:

Get to = Optimism + Gratitude + Aspiration

Your approach to living will radically improve with this expression of wisdom.

BEHAVIOR

Wisdom seeks to align our beliefs and direct our mindset, but it also informs our behavior. Someone on the path of wisdom will ask this third question, which is based on behavior: *How does my behavior reflect wisdom?* It is important to answer this carefully.

Your behavior might reflect your beliefs or your integrity. It may even be a product of your intelligence or your code of conduct. But does it reflect wisdom?

Your behavior will reflect wisdom if *observation* and *intention* influence it. You observe your own behavior and you resolve to change it using strategy. How do we observe ourselves? We do it either in an open–minded way or in a self-interested way.

OBSERVATION

Open–minded observation of yourself is the skill of observing your behavior without the biases of your own self-interest. You do your best to take a neutral stance and view your behavior without defending or condemning it. You judge it not just according to the standards of right and wrong, but also according to whether that behavior is effective or ineffective.

Self-interested observation, on the other hand, assesses your own behavior according to your natural bias to defend your beliefs and behavior. You affirm or defend yourself with justification for why you do what you do. You may even condemn yourself for behavior that is contrary to your standards. Self-interested observation of yourself triggers emotional reaction to what you see, while open–minded observation views your behavior neutrally and prompts you to meaningful change.

Therefore, effective observation of yourself is open-minded. You see your behavior in the same way you would observe that behavior in someone else. You don't think in terms of excuses, reasons, or motivations. Those are the devices of self-interested observation.

Assessing our own behavior in a self-interested way makes positive change much harder.

We subconsciously defend the status quo. We protect our beliefs, some of which directly influence our behavior. In observing our behavior in a self-interested way and making resolutions to act more productively, we essentially ask our minds to disqualify the beliefs and behavior that they have always relied on for survival. It is extremely hard to do, sometimes impossible. The worst part is that it compounds the guilt we already struggle with from previous failures to improve.

This is why we get stuck in our ways. We often become stubborn in our views and opinions. We tend to fail to break bad habits or change ineffective life choices. We set ourselves up for failure. We can often admit that failure, but we then get frustrated by our inability for positive change. Therefore, we must shift to open–minded observation.

Open-minded observation of our behavior puts aside excuses, reasons, and motives, whether or not they are legitimate.

Instead, we merely observe ourselves as we would someone else and determine if what we do consistently or as a default course of action is really effective. Does the way you always talk to your cousin really improve your relationship? Do your go–to reactions at home actually strengthen your marriage? Has your coworker become a better team player because of how you relate to them?

If we find that our behavior is unproductive, we note it and determine what works better. This removes emotional attachment to counterproductive operational beliefs and allows us to embrace beliefs that produce effective behavior. This isn't always easy, either, but it is a far better approach than trying to alter beliefs while still attached to them emotionally.

INTENTION

Wise individuals perform open–minded observation whenever they sense there is a better approach to a given situation. However, observation alone cannot bring meaningful change. There must be intention as well. Intention is the resolve to do or accomplish something. 95FIVE views intention as aspirational and not emotionally tied to a preferred outcome, two features of the *get to* mindset discussed above.

A preferred outcome is how we want a situation to work out. We all have preferred outcomes all the time. We want our aunt to recover from illness. We desire a victory for our kid's softball team. We prefer the police officer lets us off with a warning. Part of intention, as 95FIVE applies it, is a refusal to be emotionally tied to your preferred outcome. When you are, disappointment becomes a real possibility and the suffering that goes with it.

This understanding goes beyond Jedi philosophy of the *Star Wars* universe and the Buddhist tradition it is based on. It is a matter of embracing God's will and accepting what experiences and outcomes He entrusts to us. Remember Jesus' prayer before He was arrested: "Father, if You are willing, remove this cup from Me; yet not My will, but Yours be done" (Luke 22:42).

Jesus replaced His preferred outcome (*remove this cup from Me*) with submission to the best possible outcome (*not My will, but Yours be done*). We should do likewise. Jesus was intentional. We should be too.

The dynamic nature of wisdom brings beliefs, mindset, and behavior to the function of effective strategy. We create ways to increase our effectiveness in our relationships, which in turn brings growth. Wisdom loves personal growth. It brings relational growth with God, your family, and everyone else in your life, as Jeremiah noted when he wrote, "Let us examine our ways and test them, and let us return to the LORD" (Lamentations 3:40 NIV).

Why is it important to examine ourselves through the scope of wisdom? We will discuss that in the next chapter, where we will look at relationships and pressure.

YOUR STRATEGY

1. Move your mindset to *I get to*
2. Learn to observe your behavior with an open–minded approach
3. Be intentional by seeking the best possible outcome

3

WHAT BRINGS OUT THE ME
THAT PEOPLE SEE?

Pressure and How it Affects You
and Those in Your Life

*And if one can overpower him who is alone, two can resist him. A
cord of three strands is not quickly torn apart.*
(Ecclesiastes 4:12)

This chapter will show you:
- Where the battlefield of your life challenges really exists
- How to understand the real "you"
- The true nature and purposes of the difficulties you face

95FIVE is about relationships. We are not a relationship "program"
but an approach to self-assessment that will translate into healthier
relationships. You may be thinking, "Relationships are great, and I want to
have better ones, but I need to fix myself first."

We would ask people with that perspective a couple of questions:

1. How many books, CDs, sermons, programs, and retreats have you participated in that were designed to repair or realign your inner self so that you can be more effective with others?
2. Did they work as expected?
3. How healthy are your relationships now?

As for the third question, we aren't asking how conflict-free your relationships are, or how much you are benefiting from them. We urge you to consider how healthy they are. There is a difference between peaceful relationships and healthy ones. Healthy relationships are ones that grow stronger and develop qualities that are beneficial not only to you both, but to others as well.

The inside–out approach we generally pursue to improve ourselves only works to an extent. There is a "battlefield of the mind" that you have probably heard of. It is a very important battlefield, and we talk about it in our teaching, as you will see in this book. However, there is another battlefield in life where you must contend with your challenges and problems. It is the battlefield of your relationships, and it is connected with your mind, where you fight your inner battles.

Do all your problems exist in the theater of your relationships? They do, considering that you have a relationship with yourself. You also have one with God, who knows our hearts better than we do. We believe, then, that life is composed of relationships. Your life is your relationships, the ones you have with God, yourself, and other people.

95FIVE categorizes relationships into eleven groups:

- God
- Self
- Spouse (including engaged persons)
- Children
- Family (members of your household other than your spouse or children)

- Extended family (relatives and in-laws)
- Place of worship
- Career (anyone you work with, including bosses, employees, coworkers, vendors, customers, board of directors, etc.)
- Friends
- Community (associations, clubs, unions, lodges, activist organizations, affinity groups, neighbors, etc.)
- Pets (animals are important to many people and can be affected by our challenges, just like any other relationship)

Most tend to have the belief that relationships are a very important part of life. 95FIVE believes that they *are* life. We inhabit a world of relationships created by God, who is relational. That is key: God is relational.

As far as we know, there is not a verse in the Bible that says, "I, the Lord your God, am relational." We know He is, however, based on what He has created, and how prevalent relationships are in His word. Why, though, does an eternal, all-powerful God decide to create a species with whom He can have a relationship? Was He lonely, as a lot of Bible teachers have suggested over the years?

The answer is that He has never been lonely. He doesn't need humankind, or any other of His creation, either. The best way to handle the concept of God and relationships is to admit that you can never fully understand it, because you are not eternal like God is.

Our existence is bounded by space and time. We can only be in one place at a given moment. Furthermore, we have a beginning and an end. So does everything else. Even angels had a beginning. However, that is not true about God.

We view everything in terms of beginning and end. We witness it every day. Babies are born and grow up. Grandparents and parents eventually die. The same goes with animals and plants. Even billions–of–years–old stars and planets have a birth and death. Activities, thoughts, songs, and movies also are limited to beginning, middle, and end. That is how God created life.

No one created Him, though. He is ever-existent, and so are His purposes. Everything is "now" to Him. Therefore, we cannot think in terms of a point in history where He decided to enter into a relationship with a part of His creation: us. The determination to be in relationship is a part of His nature and thus is as eternal as He is.

God made us in His image, and even though we have marred that image with sin, we still bear qualities that depict His nature. He made us as relational beings and ordained that we be organized into relationships. These relationships were meant to reflect God's character, and that fact alone should motivate us to pursue healthy ones. Let's look briefly at how each relationship from our list can reflect God.

GOD

Being in relationship with God fulfills the primary purpose He has for humanity. Not having this relationship leaves a terrible emptiness within us and keeps us bound to the universal penalty of sin, which has affected all of us.

SELF

We can have a relationship with ourselves because we were made in God's image. We can know and communicate with ourselves. We can learn in ways other than just by the instinctive stimulus/response manner that conditions the behavior of animals. Science identifies humans as beings who have self-awareness, which elevates us above animals. I am aware of myself in a way that my dog is not. Neither is your goldfish or the cows you see in the field when you drive in the country.

SPOUSE

What is the purpose of marriage? Reproduction? No. Reproduction is the function of sexuality that is to be confined to marriage, of course, but the purpose of marriage is stated by the apostle Paul. In speaking of marriage, he explained the roles of the husband and wife, particularly how the husband is to love his wife in the same way Christ loves His church (His bride). "This mystery is great," he concluded, "but I am speaking with reference to Christ and the church" (Ephesians 5:32). Marriage reflects in the most powerful way the union that Christ has with His people.

CHILDREN

Our kids populate the earth and carry on after we are gone. It is a great responsibility to raise children and a critical service of stewardship to exercise guidance over their souls during their upbringing. How does this relationship reflect God's character? By showing how He is intimately and intentionally involved in extending His glory by working through His church to bring His salvation to those who do not yet know Him. Having and raising children is a picture of the united work of God and His people to reproduce His character and love in others. For those who adopt children, the picture has a further brilliance in representing how we all are adopted into Christ's family.

FAMILY

Spouses and children are members of your family, of course, but in a more extended way, so are those who live in your household who are not your kids. You might have aging parents living with you, or grandchildren, or perhaps a relative. Some households have non-related members living under one roof. What a picture of the church that is! We are a collection of ethnicities, talents, ages, backgrounds, knowledge, and even individual expressions of spiritual gifts. Sometimes it is a challenge to cooperate with each other, but when we learn to love each other as Christ loves us, we represent His wisdom and nature to the world.

EXTENDED FAMILY

Our extended families are extensions of us. We share genetics and memories, among other blessings. When we are good to our relatives, we celebrate the power of kinship, a wonderful reality we enjoy in His kingdom among all of our brothers and sisters in Christ. Just as God has brought Himself together with His people, and He brings a husband and wife together in the most godlike relationship on earth, so He brings two extended families together. He makes the earth richer with the kinship enjoyed by individuals with their extended families. Jew and Gentile alike enter together in covenant with God through the blood of Christ.

PLACE OF WORSHIP

I was glad when they said unto me, Let us go into the house of the Lord. (Psalm 122:1 KJV)

Both Daniel and the apostle John saw a vision of innumerable people before the throne of God (Daniel 7:10; Revelation 7:9–10). What they saw as completed is what we see now as countless congregations and Christian gatherings around the world. God loves the worship of His people. He knows that our worship is hindered if we do not gather and serve in unity. Your relationship with your fellow church members is a reflection of the unifying power of God to bring people of all backgrounds to the foot of His throne.

CAREER

Our workplace relationships reflect our stewardship of the earth. It is entrusted to us to care for and to cultivate to yield life–giving resources. Our first parents, Adam and Eve, worked in partnership to care for the garden in which they were placed, and their descendants have done the same, from their children to all the tribes and nations that have inhabited the earth since. We honor the work and creativity of God when we develop strong work relationships.

FRIENDS

The blessings of friendship are second only to those of marriage and children. God gave us the capacity to knit our souls with individuals who share our lives. Friendships are forged for many purposes and in countless circumstances, but good friendships are hard to break, as Solomon wrote, "A friend loves at all times, and a brother is born for adversity" (Proverbs 17:17). Friendship with others reflects our friendship with Christ.

COMMUNITY

The Lord has a mission for us. Share His love and His word. We must be ready to do that in any relationship, but our community is a symbol of the world in need of Christ. Whether it is a social organization or the people who live on your street or in your apartment complex, your testimony waits to shine bright in these places. The relationships we have with those in our community represent the loving and caring nature of our creator, who calls out to a lost world. We are his representatives.

PETS

Why do we consider them an important relationship that reflects God's character? The Bible contains a story that the prophet Nathan told to King David in the aftermath of his sin with Bathsheba. Featured in it was a poor family who had a pet sheep that was like a family member to them. That was an acknowledgment of the reality of pets, even in those times (2 Samuel 12:1–4).

Adam and Eve had a special relationship with their field animals and must have been horrified when God killed some of them to make clothes to cover the human couple's shame. Sheep, goats, and cattle were given to

Israel for sacrifice, which were represented beautifully by the final sacrifice made by Jesus for our sins. Pets symbolize the patient and gentle love God has for us in how we pour out our love for lower creatures. The loyalty and dependency they show to us in return is a great picture of how we ought to respond to God for all He does for us.

Relationships are important. We all have them. If you are a hermit living alone in the woods, you have a relationship with yourself, and we hope with God, too. The rest of us have some or all of the relationships listed above. Our job is to exemplify God in the ones we have.

Relationships are also important because they are where pressure hits us. Your challenges affect not only you, but often someone else as well.

- Trouble at work affects how you relate to your spouse and children when you get home
- A crisis confronting your friend affects your emotions, as well as those of their family and other friends
- An angry, rebellious teenager distracts you in the workplace because of all the pain and worry they inflict on you

Financial problems, job loss, car repair, illness, marriage hostility—all these and more are examples of how pressure comes to you. The technical term for how pressure engages something is insult. 95FIVE borrows that term from the field of physical science to describe how pressure interacts with people. We all bear the *insult* of pressure at times and to varying degrees, including in our relationships, which themselves can cause pressure, or pressure can affect them directly and us indirectly. Either way, the reality of pressure is a part of life for everyone.

Where your character comes in is how you manage your pressure. Pressure reveals who we really are. The battlegrounds where we contend with pressure are in our minds and in our relationships. We tend to define ourselves by what is in our minds and hearts. Others define us by how we act.

Our relationships are the arena
where we are exposed for who we are.

95FIVE believes the real you is the one that is shown by your actions. Behavior tells the truth about the alignment of our higher beliefs with our operational beliefs. We define ourselves by our higher beliefs. Others see the true definition of us by the manifestation of our operational beliefs in our behavior.

Jesus was brilliant when He internalized sin, using adultery as an example. He taught that lusting after someone made a person just as guilty of adultery as he if they committed it physically. Why did Jesus teach this? Because He understood that our operational beliefs tell the tale of who we really are, even if our outward behavior doesn't express them. They at least are manifested by internal behavior, the thoughts that we entertain, which both we and God can see.

Therefore, we suggest you ask yourself, using the open–minded assessment of your behavior we described in the last chapter, *What does my behavior tell others about me?* If you are honest with yourself, this can be a challenging and revealing discovery.

What Does Behavior Include?
- Your actions
- Your facial expressions and body posture
- Your conversation
- Your listening skills (or lack thereof)
- How you engage with others
- The way you react to circumstances or behaviors of others

With each of these types of behavior, you can ask questions about what they might be communicating to people. For example:
- What is my resting facial expression?

- How do my actions communicate to others my faith and convictions?
- Do I show genuine interest or concern when others speak to me?
- Do I look disinterested, timid, arrogant, or confident when others see me?
- What emotions do I show when confronted with difficult circumstances?

Certainly you can think of other questions to ask yourself. The more rigorous we are with this kind of self-examination, the better we are at understanding how we come across to others. This leads to positive behavioral change.

Keep in mind that pressures are not just negative forces that challenge us. They can be positive as well, and equally challenging in how we manage them.

WE FEEL POSITIVE PRESSURE FROM EVENTS SUCH AS:

- Getting a job promotion
- Going to college
- Having a baby or adopting a child
- Joining a new church
- Relocating to another town or city

Whether positive or negative, life is a pressure–filled adventure. How do you act in response to it? Better yet, how will you respond to it after learning some relational and emotional skills? Start with switching to a *get to* mindset and begin learning the skill of open–minded assessment, as we talked about in the previous chapter.

Then learn, as a person of faith, how you can express God's qualities and love in each of your relationships. God puts you in your relationships, and He allows pressure in your life so that you can shine as His child and representative.

> In this you greatly rejoice, even though now for a little while, if necessary, you have been distressed by various trials, so that the proof of your faith, being more precious than gold which is perishable, even though tested by fire, may be found to result in praise and glory and honor at the revelation of Jesus Christ. (1 Peter 1:6–7)

In the following chapter, we will look more at the nature of pressure and how it affects us. You will discover the two possible routes you can go to manage the pressures you face and which one produces authentic growth.

YOUR STRATEGY

- View your relationships in light of how they are to reflect God's character
- Consider how you come across to others by your behavior

WHAT IS MY GO–TO STRATEGY FOR PRESSURE?

Reacting vs. Responding

For God has not given us a spirit of timidity,
but of power and love and discipline.
(2 Timothy 1:7)

W*hat is my go–to strategy for pressure?* Ask yourself this question as you read through this chapter. You are about to learn a powerful shift in your approach to how you manage pressure so that its effects on you will not be as damaging as they could be. While many people are being knocked down and damaged due to how they handle their challenges, you will learn to stand strong. What is this shift? *Learning to respond to pressure instead of reacting to it.*

Making this change will not remove all possibility of emotional pain; nothing can do that. As we saw in the previous chapter, God uses pressure to test and refine our faith. However, He does not lead us to ineffective pressure management, either. He wants victory for you because He already has it, as John reminds us when he writes, "In the world you have tribulation, but take courage; I have overcome the world" (John 16:33).

To understand this shift from reacting to responding, let's look at pressure a little more closely. Have you ever heard statements like:

- This problem is really weighing on me
- I'm all twisted up inside
- Don't get all bent out of shape
- My boss is really grinding my nerves

This is the language of pressure. It also describes stress. Usually, when we think of our problems or challenges, we refer to the stress that comes with them. Stress is such a problem that adults lose sleep over it, most employees are troubled by it, and too many college students contemplate ending their own lives because of the stress and anxiety they experience.

It seems that most programs designed to help people emotionally concentrate on stress, many offering plenty of techniques to alleviate or control it. Stress affects our lives, our mental condition, and our physical health. It can be a big problem. No doubt you are experiencing it on some level.

Where does it come from? Pressure. In the science of physics, there are four categories of forces that act upon physical material: pressing, pulling, bending, and shearing. The first three types of force are self-explanatory. Shearing pressure comprises grinding and cutting. A category of shearing pressure is twisting.

When one of these pressure forces acts against a material, it resists the pressure the best it can. If a weight is placed on a wood plank, for example, the wooden material of that plank provides a sort of counter pressure to push back on the weight. If the plank is thin, and the weight placed on it is an iron anvil, the pressure will be too great for the wood to handle and it will break. If the wood is thick enough, it can hold up the anvil with minimal bending.

The strength of a material is its ability to resist pressure. If there is not enough strength, damage will occur, which may be temporary or permanent. If the pressure is too great, the material will break. A material's strength is measured by how much pressure it can resist and at the cost of how much damage. This resistance of the material is called stress.

We can say that:

- The force is pressure. Resistance is stress.
- Pressure is external. Stress is internal.
- Pressure threatens structural change. Stress tries to defend against structural change.

Interestingly, the pressure and stress we face works much the same way. You have the pressure of earning a living and caring for your friends and loved ones. Sometimes, extraordinary pressures come against you, such as illness, job loss, or a major life event that excites you. It all brings added pressure to you and the ways you attempt to handle that pressure are your stress.

Pressures come from the outside—other people, unforeseen events, harmful circumstances—and your coping methods are you pushing back at the pressure. Your stress, that pushing back, is internal. There is one difference, though, that differentiates you from a wooden board or a lump of putty: you have the unique ability to put pressure on yourself. You can give yourself stress.

Therefore, pressure is mostly external, but it can also originate internally, which makes your stress much greater. It is unfortunate, but we tend to partner with the pressure that makes us miserable by adding to it and fighting against it at the same time. Humans are interesting creatures!

We do much better when we take another approach. No, you can't get rid of stress, but you can lessen its effects on you. We gain more effectiveness by leaving our coping mentality and moving to a management mindset. Those who are in a coping mentality try to deal with the pain of their stress.

The individuals who opt for a management mindset handle their stress by more effectively managing their pressure. If external pressure can only be managed a little bit or not at all, you can learn to exercise control over your internal pressure. You will still have stress, which isn't always harmful, but you can channel it more effectively when you begin with managing your pressure.

Your ability to learn this approach begins with an understanding of reacting and responding to your pressures. Shifting from reacting to responding has the potential to dramatically reduce your ongoing stress and give you more joy in negotiating the many challenges of life. "Consider it all joy," James told his Christian readers, "when you encounter various trials" (James 1:2). It is very difficult to have joy when you are coping with stress. But when you learn pressure management, when you learn to respond to challenges, you develop joy as you see the higher purposes and opportunities in your pressures.

So then, let's look at the concepts of reacting and responding. Admittedly, this may sound like semantics. Both words are used interchangeably in normal conversation. We define them in different terms for describing the two different approaches to managing pressure. Please keep in mind that these are our definitions of the words.

REACTION

Reaction, in our view, is an instinctive and emotional way to think and act in the face of pressure. Not all reaction is ineffective or inappropriate. You would certainly react if a toddler were about to walk onto a busy street, for example, or you would run from something that endangers you. That is a natural reaction to a threat to you or someone else. It is the "fight or flight" response to danger that psychologists talk about.

As for the normal life pressures that affect everyone and the unexpected blindsides life hits us with, we need to consider whether reaction is the appropriate way to manage those pressures. Ask yourself these questions about the pressures you have right now:

- What are the pressures that threaten my peace or emotional well-being?
- Am I managing them with the force of my will or the power of my emotions?
- Is it working?

Life has a way of sending issues our way that knock us off balance or threaten our emotional stability. An emotional strategy to handle your challenges is ineffective beyond managing an immediate threat. Two painful results come from such a strategy:

1. You prolong the original emotional state.
2. You add further emotional chaos by introducing other emotions to fight against the feelings you have retained from the moment the pressure hit you.

It is important to keep in mind that there is a difference between having emotions and developing a strategy based on emotions. If you are diagnosed with a serious illness, for example, you are going to experience great anxiety while sitting there listening to the doctor tell you what is going on in your body. After you walk out of the clinic and drive home, you retain that anxiety and probably experience fear as well. It's natural!

However, you will need to develop a strategy for how you will manage the ongoing illness, from following the doctor's medical counsel for therapy and pain management to the personal issues relating to matters such as relationships and finances. Your illness will affect more people than just you. How will you handle those issues?

However you choose to manage your illness, you will continue to experience the fear and anxiety you felt at first. Who wouldn't? A wise person, however, will resist creating a strategy based on those emotions. A reactive person will descend further into those emotions and create additional pressure for themselves. External pressure and internal emotional pressure combine to work against their well-being. That compounds the stress they will experience.

Additionally, when the reactive person has moments of clarity when they realize the emotions they develop are counterproductive, they resort to a commitment to fight against them. For instance, if the person with the critical illness realizes along the way that fear, intimidation, anger, and self-pity are keeping them in emotional chaos, they will engage their determination and willpower to counter their emotional state. Unfortunately, their determination will call upon other emotions to bring them to a more positive mindset.

What does this do? It pits preferred emotions against survival emotions. The mind wants to feel anxiety and fear because that is what it believes will move the person to action. Those will be the emotions the subconscious holds on to while the conscious struggles against them with contrary emotions. It is a sort of *want to/have to* conflict in their mind.

The damage this does to our sense of well-being includes big doses of discouragement when we fail to overcome our reactive emotions with more positive ones. Enough discouragement can lead to despair, hardly a helpful frame of mind when battling formidable pressures such as critical illness, financial crisis, or the breakdown of a significant relationship.

Some may argue that we should replace negative frames of mind with positive ones. 95FIVE agrees. We should. However, the operative word is *replace*. What reactive persons do is struggle. They struggle against the negative emotions rather than replace them. To understand the difference, let's look at responding as an alternative to reacting to pressure.

RESPONDING

Responding to pressure takes a more productive and effective approach to managing pressure than reacting does. Remember, a reactive strategy:

- Is meant for initial responses to a threat
- Is emotion-based

- Produces inner pressure to add to the insult of the external pressure
- Skews our view of the reality of the situation
- Creates unproductive stress

Adding to this list is the tendency of a reactive approach to make future pressures even more difficult to manage if you continue with reaction with those pressures. A responsive strategy actually has the potential to make your present pressure and future pressures less impactful on your emotional well-being. Learn the strategy of response now, and you will be better equipped to manage your challenges from now on.

Responding is not a difficult approach per se, except that we often must implement it despite our survival emotions. That is challenging, especially at first, but soon such a strategy shows its wisdom as you see the transformation of your stress from unproductive to productive. You will feel more in control and not so helpless under the weight of your pressure. Instead of fighting your pressures and crises with emotion, you fight it with strategy.

Strategy is at the heart of response. You take a proactive and intentional approach and manage it to the best of your ability. We believe that strategy relies on answers to the following questions:

- What is the exact nature of my pressure?
- What useful information is available to me about the pressure?
- What internal pressure have I created that adds to my stress?
- What parts of the pressure can I control?
- What triggers me to react emotionally to the pressure rather than stay faithful to my strategy?
- What steps can I take to address the part of the pressure that I can control and manage the parts I cannot?
- What sources of help should I pursue to assist me with this pressure?

Remember, pressure comes in the form of problems, conflict, challenges, adventures, crises, and even tragedy. Sometimes our pressures result from previous choices we made, and at other times they are totally outside of our influence. Either way, we are affected. The first thing to do is to resist second guessing why our pressure happens or resenting how unfair it might be. Instead, we ask our questions.

WHAT IS THE EXACT NATURE OF MY PRESSURE?

Think of one of the primary pressures you are dealing with now or have recently. What would you say it was? Often we fail to address a problem or issue because we are vague about what it is. Statements like these are unhelpful:

- Everything is so crazy right now.
- I'm too busy to get the important things right.
- My husband is being a jerk these days.
- I can't seem to wrap my head around my responsibilities anymore. It's all getting away from me.

These are serious issues, to be sure. In your head, they may be specific enough to know what your pressure is, but it could also be that you are frustrated at symptoms of your pressure without understanding the underlying cause of those symptoms. The more specific your identification of the issue, the better your strategy to manage it.

Look at these examples again, this time in a more specific way.

- Everything is so crazy now *because the added demands of my job are distracting me from organizing the rest of my life.*
- I'm too busy to get the important things right *because I have recently accepted more volunteer responsibilities than I can probably handle.*
- My husband is being a jerk these days. *I'm not sure why, but he has been blindsided by accusations from his best friend of*

doing something serious that he did not do, despite the evidence we both provided of his innocence. He has serious trust issues right now, and he is probably acting out his disappointment and frustration.

- I can't seem to wrap my head around my responsibilities anymore. It's all getting away from me. *My mother's cancer diagnosis has me tormented with worry and grief.*

When we look behind the symptoms so that we pinpoint the true, or at least probable, cause of those symptoms, we can get a specific definition of the actual problem or challenge.

With an accurate diagnosis, we can devise a more relevant strategy to manage our pressure.

Obviously, some pressures present themselves specifically enough. We don't have to hunt for them. "I'm forty-eight years old and I just lost my job at a company I've been with for twenty-five years" is a clear-cut pressure. Other pressures need to be identified by looking behind their symptoms.

WHAT IS USEFUL INFORMATION ABOUT MY PRESSURE?

This comes in two forms:

1. Information about the nature of the pressure
2. Information about the possible removal or lessening of the pressure

Information about the nature of the pressure is very useful. Generals about to go to war learn as much as possible about the enemy. Coaches study their next opponent to learn as much as they can about the other team. Knowing as much as we can about our pressures can educate us enough to find better ways of managing them.

If you were diagnosed with a serious medical condition, research it as much as you can to learn more about it. You may learn new methods of managing it as well as being exposed to experts who have effective ways of overcoming its effects or limitations. If you have an issue with a problematic child, learn more about the behavior they exhibit and ways you can confront that behavior more productively.

Not only should you learn more about the nature of the pressure but also potential ways you can either lessen it or alleviate it altogether. You may be surprised by what you find out. You could save yourself from needless suffering. At least you can find ways to make your issues more manageable, and that is important to your well-being. Useful information may not make the pressure go away, but it enables you to have a more effective and mature approach to dealing with it.

WHAT INTERNAL PRESSURE HAVE I CREATED THAT ADDS TO MY STRESS?

This is an area where you can tap into your new open–minded self-observation skills. Think carefully about how you might be adding to your own misery. Do you scold yourself or direct disapproving insults or criticisms at yourself? Do you set impossible standards that must be met to avoid self-condemnation? Do you imagine God looking down on you, having the same disappointed expression you saw many times on the faces of your parents while growing up?

Most of us have times when we lack kindness for ourselves. It is sad, but we probably can show more forgiveness to a mugger who robbed us than to ourselves for making another mistake. Humans have a unique capacity for punishing ourselves much more severely than we should. It is unfortunate because such internal pressure distorts God's approval of us.

As the apostle Paul reminds us, "Therefore there is now no condemnation for those who are in Christ Jesus" (Romans 8:1). It can be quite difficult to do, and you may need to seek help with it, but do all you can to learn to put aside your self-criticism and disapproval and remove from yourself the internal pressure that compounds your stress.

WHAT PARTS OF MY PRESSURE CAN I CONTROL?

It is tempting to have the attitude that if you cannot conquer your pressure, then why do anything? Some individuals resort to excuses and self-justification that "empower" them to "accept" their pressure as is, without doing anything about it. They claim it is God's will, that He is testing them. They call their issue their cross to bear, or a thorn in the flesh that "God's grace is sufficient" for. They deceive themselves with inactivity.

Whether it is laziness or lack of confidence, these believers delude themselves by a lack of faith in God helping those who in obedience participate in the solution. Jacob, the great patriarch of God's people, knew a great deal about pressure. One of those times he worked for seven years as a dowry to marry his Uncle Laban's daughter, Rachel. On the wedding night, Laban slipped his other daughter, Leah, into the honeymoon tent.

When Jacob found out he was tricked, he complained about the treachery to his uncle, but what was done was done. Did Jacob sit around and accept the situation as his burden to bear from God's providence? No, he participated in the solution. He worked another seven years for Rachel.

Yes, polygamy comes into this story, but aside from that, we can learn from Jacob the determination to control the parts of our pressure available to us to change or diminish. There can be profound effects on your stress when you actively engage with the pressure rather than resist it.

WHAT TRIGGERS ME TO REACT EMOTIONALLY TO THE PRESSURE RATHER THAN STAY FAITHFUL TO MY STRATEGY?

An important factor to watch out for are those things you might see or hear that send you back into your reactive emotional state. An example might be a person who has to work two jobs to support their family, and every time they are exposed to a social media post of a friend having fun on vacation, they are driven back to feelings of despondency. Just because we decide to take a responsive approach doesn't mean we aren't vulnerable to being triggered back into our old way of thinking and feeling.

WHAT STEPS CAN I TAKE TO ADDRESS THE PART OF THE PRESSURE THAT I CAN CONTROL AND MANAGE THE PARTS I CANNOT?

This is where the mechanics of your strategy come in. We will look more at strategy in a later chapter, but think of some action steps you can begin taking right away. That is a good start. Then create a plan that will lead you toward managing the parts of the pressure you can control and the parts you have to live with for the time being. Some things you cannot change, especially other people. Learn the skill of living in harmony with what you have no control over. You have control over yourself. Your strategy should begin there. How can you change to be more effective?

WHAT SOURCES OF HELP SHOULD I PURSUE TO ASSIST ME WITH THIS PRESSURE?

There are countless resources available to help us negotiate our pressures and challenges. Included in these are helping professionals who want to show you methods and strategies to enable you to get a better handle on your pressure. Whatever resource you choose, it should be aligned with the belief that you are responsible to do what you can to manage your issues; they will not leave on their own. If they do for some reason, others will take their place and you will end up in the same rut if you don't learn to be responsive and strategic.

It is critical that we make the switch from reacting to responding regarding pressure. It makes a big difference. People who respond will still have problems and the emotions that go with them, but they certainly are better off emotionally and more effective in their lives and relationships.

Next, we will look at the common strategies most people use in reaction to their pressures. We have our default settings that create behavioral patterns that are exhibited when we come under pressure. These will be described in the following chapter.

YOUR STRATEGY

- Learn the difference between pressure and stress
- Shift to a responsive approach to pressure rather than remaining in a reactive mode
- Become accustomed to asking yourself the pressure response questions described above

5

WHAT IS MY DEFAULT STRATEGY FOR MANAGING STRESS?

The Many Faces of Reaction

Unless the Lord builds the house,
They labor in vain who build it;
Unless the Lord guards the city,
The watchman keeps awake in vain.
It is vain for you to rise up early,
To retire late,
To eat the bread of painful labors;
For He gives to His beloved even in his sleep.

(Psalm 127:1–2)

I n the last chapter, you learned of the significant difference between reacting and responding to pressure. We are going to continue with that in mind in this chapter, only this time we will look at the several manifestations of a reactive approach to pressure and how they try to relieve our resulting stress. You will learn:

- How you might be jeopardizing your success in life by being reactive
- How you can fight your battles and participate in the solutions to your problems while still living in faith
- What you can do now to change how you handle your stress

Stress is a critical issue. It is a familiar term in society because it is the face of pressure to many individuals. Even without a full understanding of pressure, we all know what stress feels like. It can give us an overabundance of adrenaline. It often makes us feel like our stomachs are twisted up in knots. We become overly sensitive to everything that comes our way, even the minor pressures, and we remain tensed up in our muscles. Stress even contributes to high blood pressure and ulcers.

While this isn't a book about stress management, 95FIVE understands that stress is at the heart of the emotional pain individuals often feel. We also realize that stress is both natural and essential. The culprit behind our emotional and physical misery isn't really stress; it is *mismanaged* stress. We mismanage stress by not properly managing the pressure that causes it.

Mismanaged stress has two particularly negative effects on us:

1. It makes having faith very difficult.
2. It makes having healthy relationships very difficult.

How can we have faith in everyday life if we remain captive to mismanaged stress? What adds to the confusion in our thinking and emotions is that we truly believe in the reality and power of God. So why doesn't that translate into having rock–solid faith that the Lord will address the individual problems we face? We remain fearful that our problems won't be solved and in fact will become worse, even though we don't have a good doctrinal reason for feeling that way.

This problem, we believe, is rooted in our tendency to have distorted or unrealistic expectations of ourselves. How so? Here are some reasons:

- We feel unworthy of the Lord's assistance.
- We misunderstand our role in the solution to our problems.
- We lack faith in ourselves.

Feelings of unworthiness are common enough in nearly everyone's Christian experience. It isn't about being unworthy of forgiveness and salvation, which we all are, but about being worthy of His ongoing care and provision. As God's children, though, we were made worthy of His care for us by Christ, yet we still convince ourselves that He will take care of other people's problems, but not our own. It is a rather self-defeating spiritual mindset.

Even more damaging are the distorted ideas concerning how we are to be involved in the solution to our problems. Either we take the route of anxiety and take matters into our own hands, leaving out the potential for God to do His work in the situation, or we take a misguided version of the "Let go, let God" route and remain completely passive, thinking that it would be inappropriate to contribute to the solution at all. Neither approach is effective.

On the other hand, if we have a reasoned understanding that God wants us to be involved in the solutions to our challenges where we are able to do so, we still might face the reality that we lack faith in ourselves to be effective. The question is, how can you be an active participant in resolving or lessening your challenges with confidence that your participation is biblical and not generated by the pride of your flesh? We suggest this simple progression of mindset:

1. I am involved, but not according to my own understanding (Proverbs 3:5–6).
2. I am involved, but only as His servant (Luke 6:46–49).
3. I am involved as a disciple who seeks to have my faith built through my challenges (James 1:2–4).
4. I am involved as one who loves to see God at work in my life and relationships (Romans 8:28).

If we allow our experiences with God during our challenges to develop our mindset to progress to the fourth stage above, we will learn to have more faith not only in God but also in who He makes us to be. Before we get to the first stage, however, we must leave the reactive default setting we have for how we manage the pressure and stress that acts upon us.

HOW DO YOU KNOW IF YOU HAVE A REACTIVE APPROACH TO YOUR CHALLENGES?

Look at the following descriptions of reactive strategy and see where you might fit in. Please keep in mind that by finding yourself in one or more of these ineffective strategies does not mean you are weak, faithless, or otherwise ineffective in life. You are still a good person, and one who loves God and the people in your life. It is important, though, to understand where you are so you can build a more effective strategy to better handle your present and future challenges.

Therefore, do not view these as a sin list, but as descriptions of how we jeopardize ourselves. God is never your enemy, but these reactive postures can make you your own worst enemy. Let's discover how to prevent doing that from now on.

AVOIDANCE

The apostle Paul observed a problem in the church of Thessalonica: some believers were living disorderly and idle lives. He wrote, "For we hear that some among you are leading an undisciplined life, doing no work at all, but acting like busybodies" (2 Thessalonians 3:11). These were probably Christians who used the church community for physical support by going from home to home, sticking their noses into everyone's business, and gladly eating the food offered to them. It was a spiritual–sounding excuse not to work. Religion is often used to avoid the realities of the pressures of life.

Avoidance, as we view it, is not just about laziness or distraction. Those are symptoms of a deeper issue, which is a reluctance to face pressures at all, hoping they will work themselves out or go away on their own. The busybody believers at Thessalonica lived in a new spiritual environment that carried with it a great deal of pressure in a culture and empire that was not sympathetic to what the Christians believed and practiced. As such, they sought a substitute they felt would relieve them of earthly pressures while still appearing spiritually minded.

Avoidance is a reactive approach to pressure and stress. When the heat of life or faith comes against us, avoidance types would rather hide from it than face it and deal with it. It is fear-based, for sure, and manifests as laziness, paralysis from anxiety, denial, indulgence, or distraction. A person who avoids present pressures is usually one who has approached pressure that way all along.

The question you might ask yourself is, *When a problem or challenge confronts me, do I confront it back with a strategic and proactive approach, or do I let the issue fester and cause me more misery?*

Do you have:

- Unanswered payment requests sitting on your desk?
- A potentially serious behavioral issue with a child you haven't addressed yet?
- An employee that needs to be terminated but who still works for your company?
- A marriage problem that is moving from simmering to exploding?
- Household projects that are stacking up?

It is easy to feel overwhelmed or be intimidated by difficult matters that demand our attention. Hiding from them gives a few moments of reprieve, but the nagging misery won't go away until we learn to respond rather than react.

DEFLECTION

Deflection is the art of turning blame or responsibility away from yourself to someone else. Some people master this art. It is part of our mental DNA. Adam and Eve, our first parents, used deflection to pass blame for their sin onto each other, Satan, and even God by insinuation (Genesis 3:9–13).

We naturally seek ways to deflect blame and guilt away from ourselves. Examples of deflection are:

- Individuals who hold up someone else as either sharing in the guilt or who cause their wrongdoing
- Those who argue their accusers are just as guilty as they are
- Ones who always have an excuse
- Individuals who always find ways to get out of their responsibilities
- People who are gifted at coming out on top of every argument, particularly where behavior is at issue
- Spouses or friends who remember everything you have done wrong in the past and use it against you if you dare point out their flawed or inconsistent behavior

Deflection is like bouncing a volleyball back over the net after it comes toward you. A good deflection question might be, *Do I take responsibility for my own actions without excuses or passing my guilt onto others?* If you have difficulty answering yes, then deflection is your go–to reaction.

The prospect of guilt is a great pressure on us. It demands we attempt to change our behavior or make amends. We often feel shame and embarrassment. No one enjoys that, and the temptation toward deflection is great for many of us. Moreover, we often use deflection to push our responsibilities or obligations onto someone else. We block the pressure of our responsibilities by sending them to other people.

BLAME

Deflection ricochets away from you the blame you know you deserve but won't take responsibility for. Blame, on the other hand, is a symptom in some people who do not recognize that they are responsible for their actions. Their behavior may have been wrong or may have brought uncomfortable consequences, but they aren't guilty in their own minds. Someone or something else beyond their control causes them to act as they do.

Blame and deflection can work hand in hand, but they are different. One important difference is that deflection is a technique or mode of operation that results from a self-justifying mindset. Blame, in the sense that we use it here, is a state of mind that manifests as victimization.

People who blame have a mindset of grievance. They hang on to their pasts and are ever alert to the unfairness of life. They blame their failures on what others have done to them, and they defend their ineffective behavior by blaming circumstances. They develop a carefully crafted narrative of themselves designed to garner sympathy from those they meet. It is usually subtle, of course, but you can discern it in their personal branding. Others who believe in their narrative are often drawn into their orbit and lend sympathy when required. These people tend to have blame narratives of their own.

Those who blame are a pessimistic bunch, but God still loves them, and they generally are great people. Their view of reality and God's providence, however, became skewed in their past, often because of misguided teaching or example. Blamers don't always avoid owning up to their failures, but there usually is some explanatory story behind them.

The Bible says, "The foolishness of man ruins his way, and his heart rages against the LORD" (Proverbs 19:3).

Blaming our circumstances, or even how the world works, is indirectly pointing a finger at God, who allows the pain and trials that confront us.

We must be careful to avoid that mindset and ask ourselves, *Do I take responsibility for my actions without blaming circumstances or other people? Even if something that affected my behavior was beyond my control, do I own what I do?* If you view yourself as you are now, and you have a litany of reasons and excuses for your present circumstances, then blame may be a reactive strategy that you have adopted.

RESENTMENT

Like deflection, resentment is often a companion of blame. Resentment sounds like a byproduct of blame, and often it is. But it also stands alone as a reactive strategy to manage pressure and stress. Blame is present in that other people or entities are blamed for our wounds and perceived disadvantages. We alleviate our sense of responsibility for our thoughts and behavior by pointing to other factors that injured us in the past or injure us still.

WE RESENT LIFE BY BLAMING:

- Abusive people in the past or present
- Ineffective teaching when we were young
- The failures of religion
- Government actions
- Racism and bigotry
- The economy
- Technology
- Our jobs

- The ills of society
- The work of Satan

These are just some of the realities that cause resentment. Like blame, resentment is very much a victimization mentality. You may actually be a victim of very serious wrongs against you, but resentment need not be a part of your story. Your grudges will not improve your life.

ASK YOURSELF

- Do I have a joyful spirit?
- Am I optimistic?
- Do I hold on to grudges against people in my past and present?
- Am I critical about nearly everything?
- Do I forgive easily?
- If I were to be honest, would I suggest to God that He hasn't been very fair to me?

Joseph's brothers victimized him, as did the wife of the man he became enslaved to. Life was very unfair to him. But in the end, when as a powerful government official in Egypt he saw the purposes of God's providence, he said to his brothers, "You meant evil against me, but God meant it for good in order to bring about this present result, to preserve many people alive" (Genesis 50:20).

An attitude such as that would free us of a negative mentality, honor God's providence, and enable us to be a blessing and positive influence in the lives of other people.

FRUSTRATION

Frustration is probably the most noticeable of the reactive strategies, although there is a form of it that others do not see as easily.

Its manifestations range from regularly blowing off steam to annoyance and even an outright angry personality. The quiet form of frustration is the habit of internalizing frustrating emotions. It may spare others from experiencing someone's hostility, but they abuse themselves with exasperation that they hold inside. Depending on where an individual falls in that range, they can be uncomfortable people to be around, even the sullen ones.

Frustration is a pressure and stress management strategy because life can be very frustrating. A perceived inability to alleviate that frustrating pressure can really grind the nerves of the frustrated person. They aren't incompetent or timid, just annoyed from having to deal with what they believe are unnecessary pressures forced upon them by the whims or shortsightedness of other people or entities.

FRUSTRATED PEOPLE HAVE A DIFFICULT TIME ACCEPTING

- People who act foolishly
- Wrongheaded government policies
- The need to compete with crowds to buy or access what they want
- Paperwork
- Uncooperative individuals
- Injustice
- Group decisions that make no sense
- Equipment breakdowns
- Illogical thinking
- Disagreement from others
- Their own limitations and mistakes

These are general examples and certainly not applicable to every frustrated person, but they represent what excites negative feelings in frustrated people. Keep in mind, everyone gets frustrated from time to time, but there are some who express frustration to deal with pressure and stress. It is their default setting.

To the frustrated individual, the Bible says, "Tremble, and do not sin; meditate in your heart upon your bed, and be still. Offer the sacrifices of righteousness, and trust in the LORD" (Psalm 4:4–5). The apostle Paul said essentially the same thing in Ephesians 4:26, citing the passage in Psalms.

Frustration is like a thermostat setting. When pressure is great enough, our needle hits that setting and we express our frustrated emotions. Greater pressures provoke more intense reactions, which over time lower our setting, meaning it will take smaller pressures to get us worked up later on. This dynamic can bring a person who is annoyed easily to a state where they are known for being cranky, a hothead, or someone who gets upset easily and clams up.

Ask yourself something like this question: *What role do exasperated emotions have in my daily reactions to various pressures?* Do you sigh in frustration? Mumble hostile words? Think bitter thoughts? Yell at others? Throw tantrums? Act aggressively? Threaten people? Think thoughts that condemn others for their actions or flaws? Feel despondent sometimes at the needless complications in life? Make yourself the center of the universe? Use passive–aggressive hostility? You may be using frustration as your strategy to deal with your pressures.

TO RECAP

- **Avoidance:** You choose not to deal with your pressures until you really have to
- **Deflection:** You manage pressure by shifting blame and responsibility to others
- **Blame:** You credit other people and circumstances for your failures when dealing with pressure and stress
- **Resentment:** You confront your pressures as an ongoing victim of life

- **Frustration:** You vent frustrated emotions in reaction to pressures

These individual reactive strategies come in various shapes and sizes. Some individuals have more than one of them, especially since they easily work together. It is important to see, however, that operating with these ineffective strategies makes healthy relationships so much more difficult.

If you find yourself in one or more of these approaches, please do not see yourself as a "bad" person, or one who is inadequate or seriously flawed. All you are doing is acting naturally according to your instinctive perception of the world. You are stuck in an inefficient reactive strategy.

Things can change, though. Ask yourself these questions when pressure comes against you:

- What is the true nature of my pressure as I am able to understand it?
- Regarding this pressure, what actions can I take that I have control over?
  - A monetary payment?
  - The fulfillment of an obligation or duty?
  - An apology or explanation?
  - A gesture of approval?
  - A car or equipment repair?
  - Using wisdom and restraint to not participate in the escalation of conflict?
- Can I address the pressure with integrity without feeling the need to judge the matter according to fairness?
- What is a more effective response other than the reaction I normally would express? For example:
  - Instead of getting frustrated, I could seek more information so I can strategically manage the pressure more effectively.

- Rather than feeling resentment for how unfair this is, I could try to see the issue from the other person's point of view.
- Instead of deflecting blame, I could analyze my contribution to the pressure.

The most important thinking shift is to avoid beating yourself up over your shortcomings, particularly if you find yourself in one or more of these general reactive strategies. Give yourself grace. Believe in the wisdom God gives you to overcome your pressures and grow in faith and understanding. Be optimistic about the future prospects of your relationships. Most people are more patient and forgiving than we give them credit for. God sure is! Just make sure you are too.

In case you wonder if your reactive strategy is all that dangerous to your relationships and emotional health, we will examine the critical results of ineffectively managed pressure on your life and relationships. In the next chapter, you will learn about relational stress fractures.

YOUR STRATEGY

- Learn the difference between pressure and stress
- Examine how you might be trying to manage your pressure and stress according to one or more of these reactive strategies:
  - Avoidance
  - Deflection
  - Blame
  - Resentment
  - Frustration
- Learn to ask productive questions about the pressures you face now

6

DO I SEE EVIDENCE OF EMOTIONAL DAMAGE IN MYSELF?

Relational Stress Fractures: The Product of Reacting

For you formed my inward parts;
You wove me in my mother's womb.
I will give thanks to You, for I am fearfully and wonderfully made;
Wonderful are Your works,
And my soul knows it very well.

(Psalm 139:13–14)

We would like to acknowledge and thank Pastor Matt Hannan, formerly of New Heights Church in Vancouver, WA, for his teaching on spiritual stress fractures, from which we developed our idea of relational stress fractures.

God made you. He expressed great creativity in fashioning you, making you into very much a unique individual, yet like all the rest of us you are created in His image. That is a remarkable realization you should have of yourself.

God is relational, as we have seen, but He still retains the authority of ownership over us, as He is our creator. Both attributes exist in Him.

- **He is relational**: He desires a personal connection to us, expressed by His deep love.
- **He has authority**: He is a sovereign God whose perfect judgment always aligns with His eternal will and purpose.

This makes our connection with God both unique and sometimes challenging to comprehend. Many individuals miss the nature of this divine/human relationship, usually by placing more emphasis on some parts of our connection with God and minimizing others. For example:

- I believe in God and get to go to heaven. He is glorified by my conversion to Him.
- I am His child and have the prerogative of access to His power and provision. My faith releases His abilities.
- I'm created only to serve God, and I will obey Him regardless of what I get out of it.

The problem with these incomplete definitions of being in relation to God is not that they do not contain truth. On the contrary, they reflect a lot of truth. The issue is that each statement of purpose is incomplete without the truths of the other statements. Each one puts emphasis on only one feature of our relationship with God. They are saying:

- I am His worshipper
- I am His child
  or,
- I am His servant

The truth is, we are all three. We were created to worship and glorify Him always, now and in the life to come. But it is also true that we become His children when He saves us. We also have the role of servant to Him— not the kind of servant who is forced, but one who serves based on the love and trust He has shown to us. Our worship, family membership, and service to God is a function of our relationship with Him.

Relationships are about common purpose. They are dynamic and function as designed when they grow and are strengthened. Some relationships exist which don't require a lot of attention, of course, but the ones that are significant to you need growth and maintenance. Your relationship with God is the most important.

You and God have a common purpose. He calls you to himself to work with Him to further His interests and increase His reputation among humanity. Literally, we are His presence on earth. It is critical that we represent His name appropriately. This is the heart of our responsibility to please Him.

Pleasing God involves worshipping Him, not just at church but every day. It is also about serving Him, and certainly about living victoriously as His child. What continues to perplex many believers, however, is why they struggle so much in one or more of these areas. You might be having challenges in your efforts toward pleasing God as well. We would like to encourage you in this chapter.

First, here are some realities you need to know if you haven't learned them already:

- **God is already pleased with you**. Your choices and behavior might not always align with what He desires, but as for you personally, He is pleased because of what Christ accomplished on your behalf (Ephesians 1:3–6).

- **Your future is as much forgiven as your past.** As adopted children, we really don't need to think in terms of past, present, and future sins. Instead, we can view ourselves as just forgiven. Period. We no longer are condemned by the penalty of violation of God's law. Jesus took that condemnation upon Himself (Hebrews 10:10–14). If you are down on yourself for your failures or behavior God doesn't approve of, keep this reality in mind. Jesus died for it. He died for the stuff you haven't even done yet.

- **There are moral implications to Christian sin, to be sure, but ultimately it comes down to Christian performance.** Is your performance as a Christian effective or ineffective? Because you were created a relational being by a relational God, you must consider this question in light of your relationships. Are you an effective representative of Christ in your relationships?

This last point is what 95FIVE is mostly concerned with. You have your spiritual leaders and your community of faith to teach you the doctrines of Christian living. However, it is our concern, based on experience and observation, that general Christian teaching focuses way more on the individual than on the stewardship of the individual in the relationships that God has entrusted to each of us.

What do we mean? The reality is that we teach individuals how to study, pray, have faith, trust in Jesus, etc. These are all good and necessary. Our relationship with God is of utmost importance. However, even though we say to those we teach in the church that loving God includes loving people, the truth is we don't teach them how, at least not on deeply meaningful levels.

Modern Christianity seems more focused on the individual experience with God and the emotional actualization that a lot of church traditions attach to it. This makes us believe that God's church on earth is missing out on tremendous opportunities to be truly missional. Yes, we have our marriage seminars and sermons on the Good Samaritan parable, but we seem ignorant of the mechanics of faith that bring the light of God's grace to our relationships.

95FIVE is convinced that it all comes down to how we manage pressure in our Christian lives, because pressure hits us through our relationships. Pressure is the training ground for spiritual growth. It is also the theater where we express our testimony of God's goodness to others.

> Therefore, since we have so great a cloud of witnesses surrounding us, let us also lay aside every encumbrance and the sin which so easily entangles us, and let us run with endurance the race that is set before us, fixing our eyes on Jesus, the author and perfecter of faith, who for the joy set before Him endured the cross, despising the shame, and has sat down at the right hand of the throne of God. For consider Him who has endured such hostility by sinners against Himself, so that you will not grow weary and lose heart. (Hebrews 12:1–3)

These verses are absolutely a statement about pressure, specifically the pressure of the Christian life. Jesus faced that pressure as well, even to the point of death (Philippians 2:8). Depending on what part of the world you live in, chances are good you will not die for your faith. But you still have the pressure of living in the spirit and example of Christ, surrounded by the cloud of witnesses watching how you manage your pressure, many of whom are your relationships.

Read through the gospel books of the New Testament and you will see examples of Jesus teaching His followers how to manage pressure. There were plenty of occasions where His disciples showed a reactive mindset, and He displayed a responsive one. His disciples had operational beliefs that serviced their survival instincts. Jesus showed that our survival is in the hands of the Father.

An example was when the disciples were in a boat on the Sea of Galilee and a storm kicked up. They were all terrified, but Jesus was asleep on the deck. They rushed over and woke Him, asking why He didn't seem to care that they were about to die. Jesus replied by asking about their lack of faith. Then He calmed the storm with His words (Matthew 8:23–27).

The disciples reacted to the pressure of the storm. Jesus responded by calming the storm and modeling the calmness of true faith. We might point out that the disciples could not have dismissed an act of nature, just as we cannot command our pressures to disappear. That is true. But God can, and that is the point of faith. Faith is a response, not a reaction to pressure.

Responding to your pressures means exercising faith.

That sounds so basic, and we are sure you have heard similar statements many times. However, it is worth repeating here because most of us get very frustrated because we often fail to express adequate faith in the face of our pressures. We want to, naturally, but we know that we do not much of the time. Then we become grieved at the poor testimony we believe we portray to our loved ones and friends, as well as to the world around us.

The question is, what do we do about it? How do we move from react to respond? We will touch on the answer to that question in this chapter and more so in the next, but part of the answer lies in understanding the potential damage you may have in your emotions and mindset. This damage comes in various forms. 95FIVE calls them *relational stress fractures.*

Relational stress fractures prevent our full exercise of faith and, as such, hinder our efforts at being pleasing to the Lord. When you understand them, you will be able to take an objective look at yourself and see where the enemy of our faith has convinced you to limit yourself from enjoying the full victory that is yours.

To make sure we clearly define relational stress fractures without giving anyone the wrong impression, here is a list of what these fractures are not:

- Spiritual strongholds of Satan in someone's life. Relational stress fractures definitely can lead to these serious spiritual issues, but they are not synonymous.

- Doctrinal error. Again, relational stress fractures can result indirectly from misguided understanding of the Bible's teachings, but they form independent of them and have more to do with our emotions and mindset.
- Mental disorders. These are clinical issues that mentally debilitate the thought process and reasoning of those who suffer from them.
- Personality weaknesses. While personality issues can influence the type of relational stress fracture someone may develop, the stress fractures themselves are another issue.

Relational stress fractures are points of weakness in our emotional well-being brought on by the excessive insult from mismanaged pressure. They happen as a result of being reactive to pressure rather than being responsive, in large part because being reactive involves adding internal pressure to that which engages you externally. Truthfully, external pressure doesn't have much power to cause these fractures, with the exception of serious trauma, in which case we are getting into the area of mental or emotional disorders.

Relational stress fractures are not disorders. They are weakened areas within us that make managing future pressure more difficult, which then makes us prone to more serious damage. External pressures, which we do not control and come from the outside, are what they are, but we can prevent them from damaging our emotions and relationships. We don't exercise that power when we are reactive.

Being reactive causes us to draw from the emotional reserves we have in other areas of life to cope with the stress brought on by pressure that hits us in a particular area. Stress at work, for example, will emotionally affect home and friend relationships. This gathering of emotional energy to fight against a pressure adds significantly more pressure to you until fractures form.

Even though these fractures exist in our emotions and influence our mindset, we refer to them as relational stress fractures because they affect the way we manage our relationships, particularly our most significant ones. They usually bear the brunt of the damage we incur from the mismanagement of our challenges in life.

What do they look like? Following is a list of the most common types of fractures with a brief description of each.

ANGER

If this is your fracture, you will feel frustration from every challenge or annoyance, however large or small it is. Your thoughts will be angry and will react accordingly to those in your relationship sphere, mostly toward those closest to you.

BITTERNESS

Bitterness fractures manifest as resentfulness. Those with this fracture believe the unfairness of life has victimized them. They resent those who hurt them and are guarded against those who haven't yet. Distrust of your relationships makes having healthy ones unlikely.

ANXIETY

Some people live with quiet dread of what might happen, because they felt helpless in previous times of pressure. If they failed to manage pressure before, they are sure they won't be competent again when faced with new problems or challenges. They believe they will let their people down during new pressure, so they live in an almost continuous state of anxiety, dreading what will happen next.

MONEY

Everyone needs money to survive in modern society. It is also fun to have enough to indulge ourselves or, better yet, to bless others with it.

However, some people find security in it. Others feel a sense of power or influence by having it. In either case, they become emotionally attached to the results of having it, so much so that they perceive it to be the cure to life's pressures. Anxiety over the lack of it can create relational stress fracture, and this can lead to dysfunction in relationships.

SEX

Like money, sex can be a source of happiness, security, significance, and even power. Mismanaging pressure by fleeing to the pleasures of sex or sensuality can fracture a person emotionally to the point where normal relationships are much more difficult. Sex is an emotionally powerful source of escape or affirmation, but its inappropriate use as a reactive strategy can create equally significant fractures within our emotional well-being.

SHAME

Shame may be among the most debilitating relational stress fractures because of how destructive it is to one's confidence. We cannot function properly in our relationships if we are chronically ashamed of ourselves. Whatever influences existed in the pasts of those with this fracture, their operating beliefs reinforce their sense of unworthiness, which is in opposition to the exercise of faith.

GRIEF

Losing what is important to you, particularly loved ones, will take you through an emotional process that is difficult and takes time to go through. It is natural, and most people have to face this challenging part of life more than once. Grief becomes a relational stress fracture when individual losses contribute to an overall sense of loss that clouds one's view of life. Reality becomes a long bittersweet drama in their minds, with sadness always around the corner. When the fracture grows in prominence, even small losses provoke grief feelings. Unresolved pressure from major forms of grief transforms into exaggerated grief emotions for smaller losses later.

DESPAIR

Despair is the feeling of helplessness and the inevitability of tragedy. Even Christians can suffer from this type of relational stress fracture, even though its essence is in opposition to the victorious message of the gospel. Like with the others, the operational beliefs of our flesh influence our outlook to the point of pessimism and a fatalistic outlook. This lack of hope and optimism is a great hindrance to healthy and productive relationships.

LONELINESS

Loneliness is the condition of feeling isolated or unwanted by others. The relational stress fracture of loneliness causes its sufferers to isolate themselves emotionally from those in relationship with them. Reasons vary. It could be the influence of other stress fractures present, such as shame or despair. It can also be a preferred existence, involving a lack of tolerance or trust in those closest to that person. This fracture makes being proactive and aspirational in seeking healthy relationships all but impossible. Whatever the influences behind this fracture, it is an emotional indulgence.

PRIDEFULNESS

We call this fracture pridefulness rather than just pride. You will learn in a later chapter some important insights about your pride. It isn't really the enemy of you or God. It has its place in your thinking process. But pridefulness is thinking and behaving in a self-centered way. As a stress fracture it can manifest in all kinds of ways, but at the heart of it, whether you are an extrovert with a type A personality or an introvert who keeps everything inside, you make yourself the center of the universe and react with outward or inward hostility to whatever challenges your sense of how everything should exist and operate. People with this fracture take everything personally and behave accordingly in ways that align with their personality.

FEAR

The stress fracture of fear is similar to that of anxiety. The difference is that anxiety consists mainly of feelings of dread, while fear is marked more by intimidation. Anxiety just knows that new pressures are always waiting just around the corner and those who suffer from that fracture keep their shields up, waiting for the next pressure to attack. Fear is not only intimidated by what is around the next corner but also by what exists now. Avoidance is the prominent strategy for these individuals because they lack the confidence to manage it effectively. The fear stress fracture in a relationship diminishes the optimism necessary to grow and take on challenges in common purpose with the other person.

ENVY

With the relational stress fracture of envy, covetousness is a primary influence in a person's subconscious operational software. Desiring the possessions, accomplishments, abilities, and blessings of others blinds one to their own gifts from God. An envious person struggles in their relationships with others and especially with God. It paralyzes them with thoughts that God distributes His favor unequally. It communicates to God that they should exist according to their own standards of being, rather than according to who God made them to be. These individuals convinced themselves in the past that they were inadequate without qualities they observed were making someone else significant to other people. Resentfulness guides their feelings and perception, and soon they struggle with relating effectively to God and the people in their lives.

We come back to the question that is the title of this chapter: *Do I see evidence of emotional damage in myself?* Perhaps you see yourself somewhere in the above descriptions. You might not be sure what relational stress fracture you have, but you know some kind of emotional issue hinders you from your efforts at pleasing God in your relationships. That is okay.

You are taking a great first step in acknowledging that something might be there. Remember that these fractures exist in varying degrees of severity, and they don't always prevent us from managing our relationships properly. However, they certainly can, particularly when continued pressure makes them worse, as we will see in the next chapter.

Please just keep in mind that these fractures can be repaired. They can also be prevented from becoming worse if you shift from reacting to pressure to responding to it. Be encouraged and don't despair that God may not approve of you because you have emotional damage. He understands and is here to comfort and guide you.

If we could urge you to do one thing right now, it would be to resist thinking of yourself and others in a good person/bad person model of judgment. It is counterproductive, especially for a person of faith. Think instead in terms of effective/ineffective. God wants you to understand that certain mindsets and behaviors are effective in pleasing Him in your relationships, while others are not.

Of course, there are implications of sin and disobedience in some of what we do that can bring emotional damage to us, and we are accountable for what we do or do not do. Again, though, your sin has been paid for. You have been redeemed and made into His child (John 1:12). Now you are being trained to be effective in His service. That is what we understand as the process of sanctification: being transformed into His likeness in how we think and act.

Jesus was great in His relationships. We can be, too. In the next chapter we will discuss the effects of continued insult from stress, which is stress concentration. It will be a very important chapter.

ARE MY RELATIONAL STRESS FRACTURES NEGATIVELY AFFECTING OTHERS?

Continued Insult and Stress Concentration

Therefore I am well content with weaknesses, with insults, with distresses, with persecutions, with difficulties, for Christ's sake; for when I am weak, then I am strong.
(2 Corinthians 12:10)

This chapter will show you how your management of pressure and stress affects others in your relationships. You will learn:

- How you sabotage yourself when you react to pressure rather than respond to it
- How you may be unintentionally hindering others from the joy and effectiveness of managing their own challenges appropriately
- The way your stress concentrates in certain parts of your life, particularly in your relationships, and makes you and others even more vulnerable to emotional pain
- Why it is critical that you shift to a responsive strategy

In the previous chapter, you learned about relational stress fractures, with a focus on how they affect your Christian living. You are called to please God with your behavior, especially as it is expressed in your stewardship of your relationships.

It is important to remember that we are creatures equipped for relationships because our creator is Himself relational.

Now let's delve into relationships and how relational stress fractures negatively affect them. You would agree that God doesn't sanction anything that brings harm to our relationships. Therefore, it is very important that we deal with our fractures so we may build up our significant relationships. It is a vital part of our stewardship of the life God entrusts to us.

As we begin, it might be helpful to review the definitions of some of the terminology we use for the sake of clarity.

Pressure: Any force that acts against our emotional well-being. It can come from both people and circumstances. It can originate from external sources or internally. There are negative pressures and positive ones. Pressure isn't bad in and of itself. It drives us to growth if we manage it appropriately. If we don't, it can bring needless pain.

Stress: Our reaction to pressure. As pressure acts against us, stress is the manifestation of our effort to act against the pressure. Stress is always internal. No one gives you stress. They can only pressure you. Your stress is what you generate in the face of pressure.

Insult: A technical term used to describe the action of pressure against an object, or, as 95FIVE uses it, a person. If a heavy weight sits on a wooden plank, the force of that weight is the insult to the plank. Cars going over bridges is an insult on the structure of the bridge. The pressures of athletic activity are an insult on the bones and muscles of the athlete. We experience emotional insults as well. Pressures of life that act against our emotional well-being are insults on our emotional structure.

Relational stress fracture: The result of continued insult on our emotional well-being. These stress fractures are weakened areas in our emotional structures that increase our sensitivity to pressure, causing us to react in more pronounced ways to even smaller pressures than we otherwise would. The vulnerability relational stress fractures create have a significant potential impact on those we have relationships with.

Now let's look at how relational stress fractures affect our people. It might be natural for you to feel that your stress fractures impact only you directly. You can bear the pain internally and hide it from your spouse, children, coworkers, friends, and everyone else. The fracture, you believe, may have indirect effects on those closest to you, but the fracture is yours to deal with privately.

Is this true, though? We at 95FIVE believe our relational stress fractures have a critical impact on others. That is why we call them *relational*, rather than emotional, stress fractures. They are a fracture in your emotions, to be sure, but they bring damage to others just as surely as they do to you. Here is why:

INTERNAL PRESSURE

Humans don't just negotiate the external pressures that come our way. We have the ability and tendency to increase their effects by adding internal pressure to ourselves. The pressure of a job loss or an expensive house repair, for example, is challenging enough, but when we react to that pressure emotionally and use our reaction as a strategy, we continue to operate in an elevated emotional state, which puts additional pressure on our emotional well-being. At this point, we cause our minds to use positive emotions and beliefs to fight against the negative ones, which come from the same source. Do you see the irony?

This internal struggle is a battle with ourselves, which is added pressure that gives more power to the external threat that confronted us in the first place. Here is where we discover a critical truth about pressure and stress. External pressures are not what cause relational stress fractures. It is your internal pressure that fractures your emotional structure. We do it to ourselves!

Extreme traumatic events overwhelm a person and damage them emotionally. In those cases, pressure is so damaging that the mind cannot defend itself from the effects of the pressure. The result is damage considerably beyond relational stress fractures and as such is beyond the scope of this book. If you have suffered from this type of trauma, we urge you to seek help from a professional equipped to guide you through the experience. You are welcome to continue reading, but please know that we must defer to the expertise of clinical professionals.

Apart from extreme traumatic events, the standard human operating procedure is to induce more pressure onto ourselves, which eventually causes fracturing. Our misguided strategy introduces continued insult upon our emotional well-being. In most cases, we have the capacity to withstand our pressures, but only if we have an effective strategy to manage them. If we don't, we risk unnecessary pain to ourselves and to others.

A good start to assessing your personal pressure–management strategy might be to ask yourself, *How am I adding to my pressure internally?* Do you maintain unrealistic expectations of yourself? Are you overly critical or judgmental of yourself? Do you exaggerate the pressure you face and stir up unnecessary fear and anxiety? Do you condemn yourself for not having the skills or wisdom to effectively address the issues that cause your pressure?

Here is another question: How would God feel about your thoughts and behavior if you treated someone else that way? Then how do you suppose He feels when you treat yourself so unfairly? If you point to your exceptional unworthiness, then you are claiming that your judgments are more accurate than His. Be good to yourself and search out those ways that you multiply your pressures and set yourself up for failure.

WE ARE CONNECTED TO PEOPLE

Another way we can describe relationships is to call them connections. Literally, we are connected to other individuals. There is a bond that forms from a common purpose in being connected to them. It can be a romantic or marital bond, parental, genetic, friendship, and even one of common interest. The bond you have with your boss is of necessity, but it still exists because your employer and you have a common pursuit. We are connected individuals.

Because of this connectedness, others will be affected by our pressures and stress. It may be a lot, or a little, but every connection we have has the potential to suffer or be blessed by how we manage our pressure. If you have a relationship with them, they share in your outcomes.

Keep in mind you have emotional bonds with people you don't have an active relationship with at the time. These probably won't be affected by your life pressures unless they are informed of them so that they may pray for you. However, ones you have active relationships with will experience some effect, whether they realize it or not.

Why is our interconnectedness so affected by how we manage pressure and stress? Think of your life as a web of relationships. You have your own individual lives, of course, but the connections make all of you vulnerable to residual effects of how each of you deal with your challenges and issues. The closer someone is to you, the more they stand to experience the consequences of your strategy. How does this work?

As we have seen, when pressure hits, we tend to react to it with stress and emotion. Worry, anger, fear, resentfulness, sadness, or resolve are emotional ways we try to manage pressure. Then we fight those emotions with other emotions in an attempt to maintain our sense of well-being. We experience pressure from its external source and from ourselves.

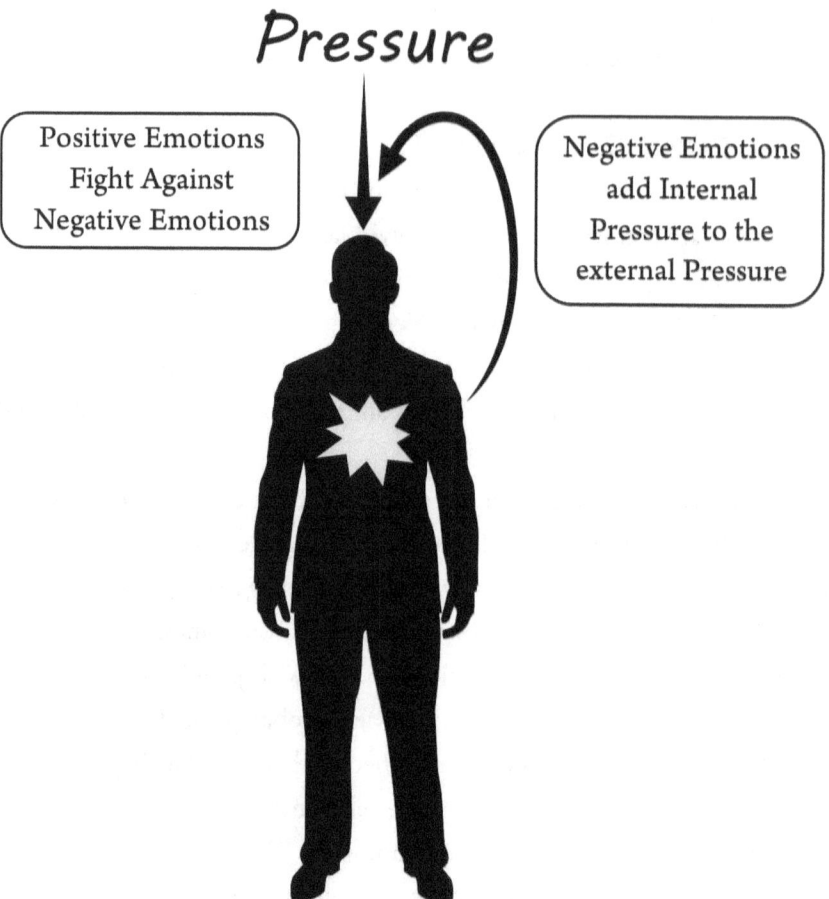

The issue with maintaining an emotional state, however, is that our emotional energy depletes, and to focus on our battle against the pressure we have to draw emotional energy from our relationships. In other words, we reserve energy we normally put into our relationships for our inner fight against the pressure.

Reactive individuals might express this function by:

- Putting extra effort into avoidance activities, such as indulging in a pleasure, which isolates them emotionally from their loved ones

- Maintaining an elevated emotional state by focusing inward with feelings of anxiety, frustration, or fear
- Expressing hostility, active or passive, toward family members or friends, because all of their kind emotions are reserved for helping them maintain an even keel when they are in public
- Nursing feelings of resentment, bitterness, or despair to the point of diminished civility to other people

There are many other ways we can manifest this, but the bottom line is that we rob those connected to us of the productive emotional energy that goes into building healthy relationships. Do not think of this process as drawing emotional energy from other people, but from our relationships with them. That distinction is important.

You cannot deplete someone's emotional energy. You can behave in such a way that they expend it on you, but they are the ones who spend it. However, you can deplete emotional energy you have reserved for the relationship by redirecting it toward your reactive efforts to manage your pressure. What does this do?

Unfortunately, while drawing out emotional energy from your relationships, you are at the same time projecting your stress upon them, because now your lack of emotional energy spent on them is additional pressure to what they are trying to manage in their lives. They wonder what is wrong with you. They struggle with angry feelings or frustrated emotions because of your neglect of the relationship. They worry about your welfare and feel left out because of your emotional isolation. That is pressure they don't need.

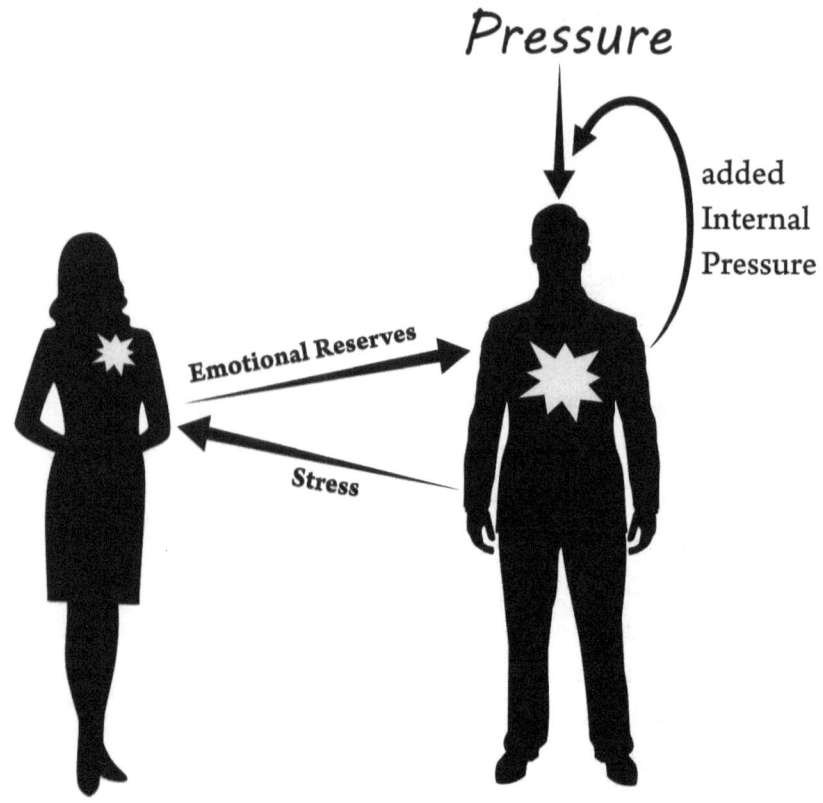

Now imagine this process taking place in all of your relationships, all due to an emotion–driven strategy of reacting to pressure, rather than responding to it.

This is why you want to avoid managing pressure and stress with emotion and coping methods. Responding is much more effective than reacting.

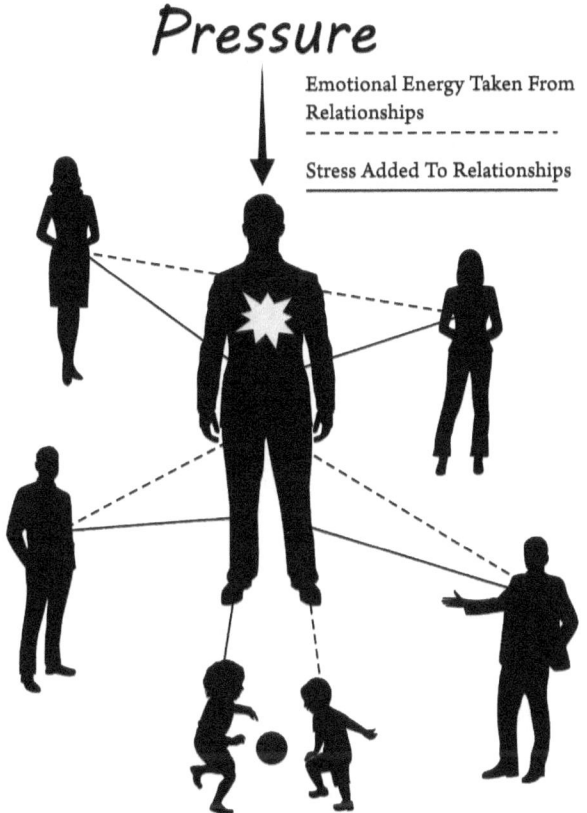

STRESS CONCENTRATION

In chapter three, we pointed out how our language and descriptions of pressure and stress are borrowed from the world of physics. We talk about being "pressed" for time, "stretched" too thin, and so forth. There is another reality in physics that has a metaphorical application to our spiritual and relational experience: stress concentration.

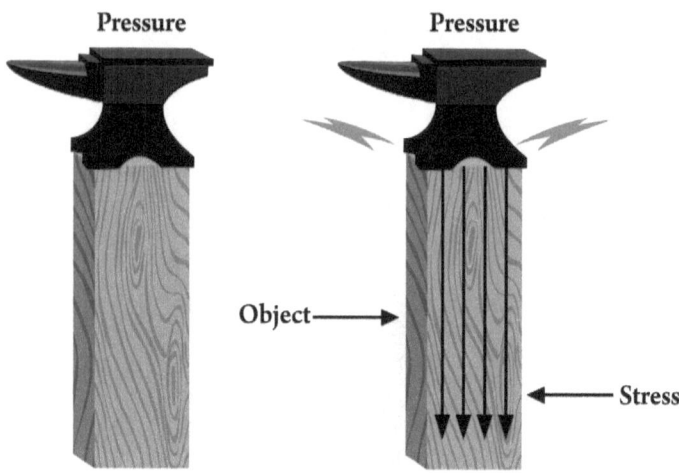

Look at this principle as it applies to pressure and stress on objects. Picture a heavy iron anvil resting on the edge of a wooden plank.

In this situation, the anvil provides pressure as it sits on the plank. How much strength the plank has will determine if it can hold up the weight and for how long. This strength is measured by its internal stress which is applied to the task of withstanding the heavy anvil.

We also learn in physics that in a material, stress flows evenly through it when pressure is applied, if there is no flaw or damage to the material.

If there is some type of disruption in the material, such as a notch, hole, or fracture, then the stress from the pressure must flow around it.

Let's say that our plank has a fracture on its side. How did it get there? From pressure. It could have developed as a result of the anvil's weight bearing down on a vulnerable spot in the plank, or a previous pressure could have caused it. It is there, however, and it has a critical effect on the rest of the material in the plank.

Without the fracture, stress from the pressure of the anvil flows evenly, as we saw above. With the fracture, however, the stress flows around it.

When it does, it concentrates in the material around the fracture, thus weakening the plank further because its remaining material is experiencing

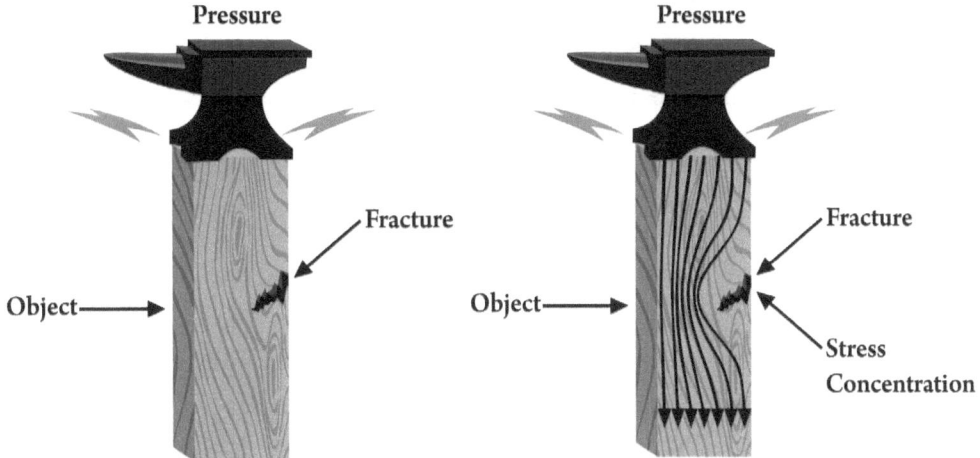

more stress relative to the weight of the anvil. The material close to the original fracture will eventually experience further fracturing, making the plank even weaker. If the anvil continues to sit on the increasingly damaged plank, eventually it will fail completely.

This is a great metaphor for how pressure and stress work upon us and our relationships. If you determine that you have one or more relational stress fractures, chances are that pressures you deal with now are triggering your stress to concentrate in other areas of your life. It isn't a physical process, as with the anvil and wooden plank example above, but it is an emotional one. Your stress concentration may be mild or severe, depending on how prominent your fracture is. One thing we know is that the fracture will increase, and the stress will become more concentrated if a reactive strategy is maintained.

How does your stress concentrate in areas of your life, exactly, and what are those areas? You guessed it—your relationships. If your life comprises all your relationships, then each one is an area of your life. That means stress concentration happens in them.

Consider the example of a man who has a lot of stress in his career. It isn't the kind of stress that results from challenges and achievements, but miserable stress brought on by conflict, poor leadership, industry problems, nagging issues with vendors, coworkers, paperwork, etc. This person reacts to the pressure rather than responding to it.

The insult from the pressure is so continuous that eventually he develops a relational stress fracture. It happened as a result of despairing over his condition and struggling frequently with depression. He fought against feelings of despondency and bitterness in an internal battle with his emotions. That put more pressure on him, and eventually the fracture in his emotional structure formed.

Now this person is more sensitive to pressures, even small ones. Whenever a new pressure emerges at work or anywhere else, he falls deeper into the emotions that caused the fracture. He is emotionally weakened and is less able to manage his pressures than he was a year ago. He feels more desperation in the face of his pressures, which adds to them. To keep his head above water, he has to use the emotional energy he normally would use for his family and friends and apply it to his internal battle.

He stops going to his daughter's basketball games. He becomes emotionally distant from his wife. Church attendance becomes less frequent and when he does go, he's in and out as quickly as possible. This person even screens calls from close friends. He constantly feels like he is circling the drain.

His post–stress fracture behavior projects his stress onto his wife, who wonders what is going on and resents being left out of his inner life. His wife even suspects unfaithfulness. His daughter is perplexed as to why one of her own parents has given up on her activities. Friends and relatives grow worried and offended that he is out of touch so often, and even when they manage to get together, it isn't much fun. The leadership at the church knows something is wrong, but they can only guess what it might be.

Each of these relationships have the person's stress projected onto them and it is concentrated stress. Effectively, they are bearing emotional burdens on behalf of their loved one. The people connected to him now have more pressure in their lives to go with what they already have to manage. This potentially weakens them further to be effective with their own issues, particularly if they are reactive as well.

Now add to the equation the likelihood that some of them have fractures of their own. Their stress concentrates around their fractures, just like our friend with the miserable work life. If, say, his wife has her own relational stress fracture, not only does he receive additional pressure from his spouse, which creates stress, but he also must contend with the emotional expenditure of reacting continually to other pressures.

They then project concentrated stress into other relationships, and if those individuals have their own fractures, well, you see how this dynamic can have plenty of consequences within the web of relationships of just one person.

You don't need to worry that your ineffectiveness in handling your own pressures will destroy other lives. It isn't like that. However, your pressure and stress–management strategy can hinder your people from being as effective as they could be in their own lives.

Therefore, if you have some cherished, healthy relationships you really want to protect, you can take a good first step by putting aside your reactive strategy and shifting to responding to your pressures. It will make a big difference in your relationships, because it will make a big difference in you.

In the next chapter, we will look specifically at what strategy looks like when we respond to pressure. A great benefit will be created when you make the shift from reacting to responding, and it will be a tremendous relationship–building resource for you. You will bless your relationships rather than unintentionally hindering them. The following chapter will teach you about the power of margin.

8

WHAT IF I COULD MANAGE MY RELATIONSHIPS DIFFERENTLY?

Switch From Reacting to Responding: The Power of Strategy and Margin

*Desire without knowledge is not good, and whoever makes haste
with his feet misses his way.*
(Proverbs 19:2 ESV)

You have learned that reacting to pressure is not an efficient way to manage it. Now we will look at two primary features of responding that will add significant value to your life if you put in the effort to keep them as part of your approach to living in relationships. The first is margin, and the second is strategy.

We have talked a lot already about being strategic, and that theme will continue in this chapter, but we will focus on the elements of an effective strategy. How do we go about having a strategic mindset and putting together sound strategies for each relationship we want to protect or build up? You will learn the four parts that should be in any relationship strategy.

First, though, we want to introduce to you another component of being responsive to pressure. We refer to it as margin. If you have margin as a consistent feature of your approach to life and relationships, you will accomplish two important results:

- You will practice wisdom
- You will have more peace in your relationships

We want to reiterate that having a peaceful relationship doesn't mean it will always be free of conflict.

Conflict, if managed correctly and in the spirit of love, can be productive.

However, a peaceful relationship will be one that is on solid ground and shielded from serious damage. Such a relationship has margin.

What is margin? It is the difference between two boundaries, two points of potential outcomes, or two numbers. The margin of a typewritten page, for example, is the space between the edge of the paper and the edge of the text. It is a difference between two boundaries. The margin of error we identify in our statistics, such as political polls, is the difference between two potential outcomes; the outcome we predict could differ from the actual outcome by a certain percentage.

Then we have margin in numbers, such as the scores of a ball game. If team A beats team B by ten points, we can say that team A won by a ten-point margin. Margin, in this case, is the difference between the two final scores.

We believe that margin needs to be a factor in our relationships. Like the examples above, our relationship margin is the difference between two or more potential outcomes of our management of those relationships, the one we want to have and the one vulnerable to damage. It is a protective cushioning, if you will, between your relationship and catastrophe, which could be defined as becoming severely damaged or broken.

You have the ability and opportunity to build margin in your relationships. It does not come naturally. The other person has that capability as well, but the beautiful thing about it is that the relationship can be improved even if you are the only one building margin.

It sounds like a great concept, but you might wonder what it means to build margin and how you do it. Actually, it is usually simple, although not always easy. The important part of building margin is that to do it you don't struggle against the issues of the other person, only yourself, particularly your own pride. If you are willing to do that, you can begin building margin right away.

Building margin begins with building credibility with the other person. This is where our pride is usually the most vulnerable. Lack of credibility is manifested by a lack of trust in you. It will sting once in a while when the other person shows lack of faith in what you say, do, or commit to doing. They might express mistrust in ways such as:

- Arguing with everything you say
- Rolling their eyes or using other facial expressions that communicate unbelief in you as someone they can trust
- Talking to you in a condescending way
- Making comments like "I'll believe it when I see it"
- Not communicating with you in important matters
- No longer asking for your help
- Using self-righteous language to claim God's will that they be careful in relating to you
- Setting strict boundaries to protect themselves from harm they feel might come from interacting with you

If one person in a relationship loses trust in the other one, it is often for a good reason and deserved. Other times, it isn't the result of the other person doing something wrong or inflicting harm, but may be due to an unintentional lapse into stagnation or emotional disconnection. It might be the person's fault who lost the trust, but they deflected blame onto someone else.

The important matter to consider is this: Is the relationship worth repairing or improving? More significantly, do you perceive it to be God's will that you preserve the relationship? If a relational and missional God entrusted people to you, chances are better than not that He would want you to put in the effort to save or improve your connections with your people.

There is another feature of margin that is important. We can find it in the verses of the Bible that describe the fruit of the Spirit: "But the fruit of the Spirit is love, joy, peace, patience, kindness, goodness, faithfulness, gentleness, self-control; against such things there is no law" (Galatians 5:22–23).

This is a margin passage of Scripture. All of these types of expressions of the Holy Spirit are listed. The margin section is the last statement: "against such things there is no law." The law of Moses in the Old Testament that informed Jewish life was the discussion of Paul's letter to the Galatian church. The purpose of the law was to train God's people with moral and ethical restrictions so they would understand the perfection and seriousness of God's righteousness.

The problem was that many individuals thought they could gain righteousness by keeping the law. Paul explained that the law cannot provide righteousness, but effectively condemns us, so that we are driven to God's grace, the true source of righteousness. In an ironic but optimistic remark, Paul lists the behaviors inspired by God's Spirit and explains that there is no law to condemn behaviors in that list and as such, those who live by them will not be condemned (see Romans 8:1). Since these behaviors (margin–building behaviors) are fully approved by God, and subsequently bring no condemnation, then it would follow that we are free to practice these fruits as much as we want. That describes the power of margin. You can't build too much of it with others. You can only bless them more and more.

Therefore, not only is margin important for struggling relationships, but it is just as critical for healthy ones as well. Margin can be lasting, but if we don't maintain credibility with our people, it can erode. No matter how loving, committed, well–meaning and faith–based you are, if you let distractions take over your attention, small but sure cracks in your relational margin will develop eventually.

The erosion may not be catastrophic, but years down the road, you might look back and wonder where you could have done better. We should be grateful for the amazing patience and grace shown to us by others over the years that sustain our relationships despite our negligence in building meaningful margin.

In many cases, we build margin with the natural expressions of love and affection we show for those we care about. Spouses do nice things for each other, and parents are loving toward their kids. Friends help each other and make each other laugh or feel comfortable. We do those things because it is what individuals do for those who they are connected to emotionally.

That is fine and well, but it is still critical to be intentional about building margin in relationships. The way we are intentional is through strategy. Strategy includes margin–building activity that is motivated by a *get to* mindset. These are founded on your beliefs.

Strategy is more challenging if your operational beliefs (mental software that informs your decision-making) are not aligned with your higher beliefs that are represented by the objectives of your strategy. For example, a spouse may truly believe in the importance of a strong and vibrant marriage, but they are lazy and motivated by taking the easiest route because comfort, absence of conflict, or convenience is part of their operational beliefs. If that spouse builds a strategy to create more margin in their marriage, it will be difficult to implement that strategy with inconsistent operational beliefs.

Therefore, it is critical to do the following when you implement a proactive margin mindset to build up your relationships:

1. **Assess the alignment of your higher beliefs and your operational beliefs.** Find your inconsistencies and draw upon God's guidance to remove them. Practice the Fruits of the Spirit until they become a stronger part of your character (love, joy, peace, patience, kindness, goodness, faithfulness, gentleness, self-control).

2. **Don't confuse strategy with objectives.** If you desire a better relationship with your group leader at church, for example, that is your objective, not your strategy. Your strategy will include the four components described below and the actions you will take to build margin with your group leader. Strategy leads to the objective.

3. **Put aside your sense of personal justice or fairness.** We cannot overstate how critical this is. It will be difficult at times because that is where your pride is involved. As long as you keep your personal code of justice active, you won't be building much margin in the relationship. Instead, you will expect the other person to do it, because such behavior on their part aligns with what you believe is fair to you. This is why relationships break down so often. If you go about your strategy holding on to what is fair to you, or why your needs must always be accommodated, you are missing the point of what it means to build relationships biblically. You don't need to be a doormat, but don't be the one who wipes their feet on it either.

Strategy is what best builds margin in a relationship. Don't rely only on the nice things you do for the other person. They build margin, for sure, but they can also be perceived as manipulation by those with whom you have lost credibility. Strategic margin–building has a much better chance of restoring or maintaining credibility and thus trust.

Look at the relationships you have now. Categorize them into the healthy ones you want to keep safe and the ones in need of attention. Remember, the strategies you create are only about what you will be committed to doing, not what you expect of the other person. If you both come together and mutually commit to agreed–upon actions and behavior, that is a covenant. But for margin-building, you are working on you. Build your character and credibility, and you stand a great chance of seeing positive changes in the other person.

How do you build your strategy? We view an effective relationship strategy as comprising the following four components:

1. Purpose
2. Inspiration
3. Accountability
4. Measurable Results

Each of these components will require us to ask relevant questions of ourselves.

PURPOSE

Purpose in strategy comprises both the objective and the mindset needed to implement the action steps of that strategy. It is where we choose to have the *get to* mindset regarding our relationships. Look at the difference between the three mindsets we talked about in the third chapter:

HAVE TO

- I better show up next Saturday to help my friend box stuff up to get ready to sell their house. That is what friends are supposed to do.

- It is my responsibility to attend church regularly. The Bible says not to forsake the assembling of ourselves together (Hebrews 10:25).
- I am required to do the best job possible at work. Being a poor employee is unethical.
- What kind of Christian would I be if I didn't accept my spouse's uncle, even though his beliefs and choices are the opposite of mine?

OUGHT TO

- I should go help my friend prepare the house to sell. I have stuff I need to get done, but they were there to help me clean up my yard last year. It's only right that I return the favor.
- It is important that I remain faithful in my church attendance. Hebrews 10:25 says not to forsake the assembling of ourselves together, "as is the habit of some." I need to be an example for others in my church.
- It is my responsibility to do the best job possible at work. I am blessed to have this job, so I should contribute positively to the company's objectives.
- I need to be accepting of my spouse's uncle, even though his beliefs and choices are the opposite of mine. That is why I am on this earth, to have a good testimony to others.

Let's look at these two approaches. Clearly, statements from both groups contain truth. There are things required of us (*have to*), and things expected of us and what we expect from ourselves (*ought to*). You can be effective in life with either of these two mindsets. However, they don't make the best strategies. Why is that? Because of a common denominator between the two: obligation.

Obligation is a part of life, for sure. It is also part of a life of faith. We all have obligations and are responsible for meeting them. However, for you to transition to the most effective margin mindset possible, learn the distinction between obligations and the sense of obligation.

Learning that distinction will help you change to a *get to* approach to stewardship of your life and relationships. The word *stewardship* enables us to switch from obligation to opportunity, from a legal way of thinking to a grace perspective.

So then, let's see how our example statements look from a *get to* mindset:

- Helping my friend prepare their house to sell is the most important thing for me to do next Saturday. It will add further strength to our friendship. Besides, the exercise would do me good.
- I understand why God wants us to be faithful in our church attendance. Hebrews 10:25 says we should not forsake assembling together like some are in the habit of doing, because we are "encouraging one another" when we meet for worship and instruction, especially when it seems the Lord's return is getting closer.
- Doing a good job at work is my chance to contribute to the economy and to build my professional skills. It is also an opportunity to represent Christ in the marketplace.
- Being accepting of my wife's uncle is both a great challenge of faith and an opportunity to learn a different perspective. He and I may never see eye to eye, but it sure would be pleasing to God for us to have a good relationship. It is the best way I can be a good witness of my faith to him.

Notice that these *get to* responses do not negate the truth of your beliefs or the conviction of your faith and ethics. They don't even remove obligation, but they transform a sense of obligation to a mindset of aspiration with your identification of opportunities in your life. You are not trying to transform reality, just your way of viewing it.

Obligation is a part of life, but when we manage our obligations with a sense, or mindset, of obligation, we add more pressure to ourselves. If we aren't careful, our *have to* and *ought to* will move us back into an emotion–driven reactive approach to managing pressure and stress. The *get to* mindset helps to keep you in a responsive management approach.

The first question to ask yourself, then, is *What is my desired outcome for this relationship, and what is my attitude in my approach to managing it and creating a strategy to build margin?* This will take honesty, of course. You might also assess how congruent your mindset is with the outcome you desire. *Will the mindset I have now increase my chances of success with my strategy, or will it hinder me?*

INSPIRATION

A *get to* mindset creates the second component of strategy: inspiration. What do you think of when you hear the word *inspiration*? Most of the time, we tend to identify inspiration in terms of performance. For example:

- She was inspired when she sculpted that tremendous work of art.
- He ran the football with inspiration, which was the greatest factor in today's victory.
- I just felt inspired to get those reports done ahead of schedule.

Inspiration is reflected in the expressions of your abilities, but the reason is that it is present in what comes before your performance: your perseverance. The home of inspiration is perseverance. The outcome is the fruit of inspiration.

The artist didn't just get overcome with a spirit of genius one day and produce her sculpture. Behind that "inspired" work of art are years of skill development and a maturing perspective on the creative and symbolic dimensions of our world. The football player had years of vigorous training and experience behind that game where his inspiration was expressed in his contribution to the victory. When you have extraordinary days at work or in your personal life when you seem endowed with an extra ability to accomplish your objectives, behind the inspiration of the moment is the inspiration of your past learning and experience.

Effective strategy has at its core the power of inspiration, the kind that exists in perseverance.

You might wonder here whether you can draw from experience and training if you are new to the idea of creating strategy for your relationships. You absolutely can! You may look back at your past and categorize your experiences like successes or failures, positive or negative. God, however, sees your past as experience to prepare you for what you are to do now.

He sees your past as an experience He has redeemed for Himself. Now He stands ready to inspire you to draw from the knowledge and lessons learned from it to apply to your work of living out His will for you. Because stewardship of our relationships reflects the stewardship of our lives to a relational God, doing His will involves being a blessing to those He gave to you. Your strategy can include the inspiration from your past as well as the perseverance you exhibit now in implementing your relationship strategies. You can say what the psalmist wrote: "It is good for me that I was afflicted, that I may learn Your statutes" (Psalm 119:71).

Your second question comprises two parts:

How do I view my past? Is it an emotional anchor around my neck, or a valuable part of my testimony?

Do I hope to get inspired when I need it, or do I embrace inspiration from my perseverance in implementing my strategy?

ACCOUNTABILITY

Like inspiration, accountability is often a misunderstood concept. It actually sounds intimidating because it conjures up thoughts dealing with strictness, unpleasant requirements, or being called out on the carpet for mistakes. Accountable relationships sometimes include these things. Unfortunately, we often project on God a posture and expression of one who holds us to strict standards that include unpleasant consequences for every failure.

True accountability is more about holding yourself to standards necessary to be effective in your relationships with others. Yes, they have expectations of you, and they should. You have expectations of them. However, the best way to ensure other people fulfill your expectations is to meet the expectations you have for yourself.

Accountability is saying, "I expect myself to perform in a principled way in my relationships, and not only will I be accountable to myself for my behavior, but I will also be accountable to the other person." In a way, that is the voice of inspiration in your relationship strategy. Inspiration expresses itself in your accountability.

Accountability is optimistic in a productive relationship. Being optimistic means your strategy will be positive and aspirational; it will pursue the best possible outcome. If you go into your strategy with a negative form of accountability—demands, conflict, punishment, legalism—then your relationship strategy will be expressed negatively. You will be defensive, which runs counter to an effective relationship strategy. Positive accountability is optimistic, and your strategy will be a living and vibrant approach to your relationship rather than a stagnant one.

Your third question: *Am I truly an accountable person, or do I only hold others accountable?* Is it your way or the highway? That is what you communicate to the other person if you bypass the critical step of making yourself accountable.

MEASURABLE RESULTS

What does it mean to have measurable results in a relationship strategy? We understand being able to observe changes in the quality of a relationship, but can results be quantified? In other words, can we really measure them?

The answer to that question is yes. We can even use literal numbers sometimes.

- We communicated in meaningful ways four times this week, as opposed to none, like it was before.
- We saved $1,000 this month after creating our financial plan.
- Ten of my employees responded positively to our new expectations agreement.

Numbers, however, aren't the chief indicator of the results of a relationship strategy. Often the results are more abstract, but every bit as real. Let's look at the beginning Scripture passage for this chapter: "Desire without knowledge is not good, and whoever makes haste with his feet misses his way" (Proverbs 19:2 ESV).

"Desire without knowledge" is kind of a strategy statement, isn't it? The verse is most likely in the context of gaining wealth, as suggested by the theme of verse one of the chapter, but the concept can apply to strategies for any pursuit, even relationships.

The term *haste* denotes an inadequate or ill–advised strategy, a reactive one. The word *haste* means to hurry or press. To press something is to apply pressure on it until it moves. The idea in this verse is to rush along with an ill–informed plan of action, which will produce unfavorable results.

The phrase at the end of the verse, "misses his way," is the measurable portion of the person's strategy. With a hasty, uninformed strategy, he will miss his way. The New American Standard Version uses the word *errs*, which speaks of mistakes or failure to achieve the objective. The King James Version uses the word *sin* (or *sinneth*, in its Old English grammar).

The Hebrew term that is behind our English translations means "to sin, miss, miss the way, go wrong, incur guilt, forfeit, purify from uncleanness,"[1] thus our English definitions of the word. Interestingly, however, the word in primitive Hebrew was represented by symbols depicting the act of using a cord to measure a distance, often by placing knots incrementally in the cord to denote units of measurements,[2] like we do with inch or millimeter marks on our rulers.

The word came to be used for sin, because when an arrow shot at a target missed, the distance was measured with a cord. The idea was that sin "misses the mark" of correct behavior. The wisdom of God is such that we can know our behavior is incorrect by how it is measured against right behavior.

In this way, not only is moral behavior "measured," so to speak, but so are the results of our strategy. The application of this principle is simple. In your relationship strategy, you can measure where the relationship is in a given metric compared to where you want it to be. Make sure that your stated objective is in alignment with what you understand God wants for the relationship.

The best part is that your objective need not be an expression of arrival, but of growth. In other words, you don't set the definitions of your outcomes in terms of an expressed end point, such as, "The outcome of my strategy will be realized when there is finally communication in my

1   Francis Brown, Samuel Rolles Driver, and Charles Augustus Briggs, *Brown-Driver-Briggs' Hebrew Definitions*, public domain, 1906.

2   Jeff A. Benner, *The Ancient Hebrew Lexicon of the Bible* (College Station, TX: Virtual Bookworm Publishing, 2005).

marriage." Instead, your objective is continued growth. "My marriage strategy will bear fruit as we continually learn to communicate better" is a growth statement.

Ask yourself, *Do I have a destination mindset for my relationships, or a growth perspective?* Do you view your relationships as a set of objectives to complete, or as a continuous series of milestones on an ongoing journey of growth? You might also begin thinking of how you can measure the results of your strategies. This will train you to notice progress and be encouraged that your strategy is producing results.

Strategies for your relationship need not always be complicated, and they certainly should not be inflexible. The idea is for you to position yourself to be more effective in your contribution to the relationship. You cannot alter the thoughts and behavior of the other person, but you can influence them. That will be the theme of the rest of the book.

You will learn what it means to have influence and what the parts of your thinking process do to determine the level of influence you have. You will also discover that, just like with pressure and stress management, a few simple adjustments to your approach can make a lot of difference. We have a relational God who is also influential. Let's learn how we can reflect him practically in our relationships.

In the next chapter, we will put all this information together and review how you can implement this way of thinking in your life.

9

HOW DO I PREPARE
TO STRENGTHEN MY RELATIONSHIPS?

Putting it all Together

You enlarge my steps under me,
And my feet have not slipped.

(Psalm 18:36)

The course of a person's life is often depicted as a journey or a path. We based this book on lessons we learned from the hiking experience of Frank, when he got lost on the slope of Mount St. Helens as daylight faded away. Therefore, let's think of hiking in the outdoors as a metaphor for how we can implement the information in the preceding chapters. We won't get lost on this trip, though, because we have our map.

We will take a pack with us. It will be furnished with what we need.

We are going to put in three essentials:

- Productive beliefs
- Advantageous mindset
- Effective behavior

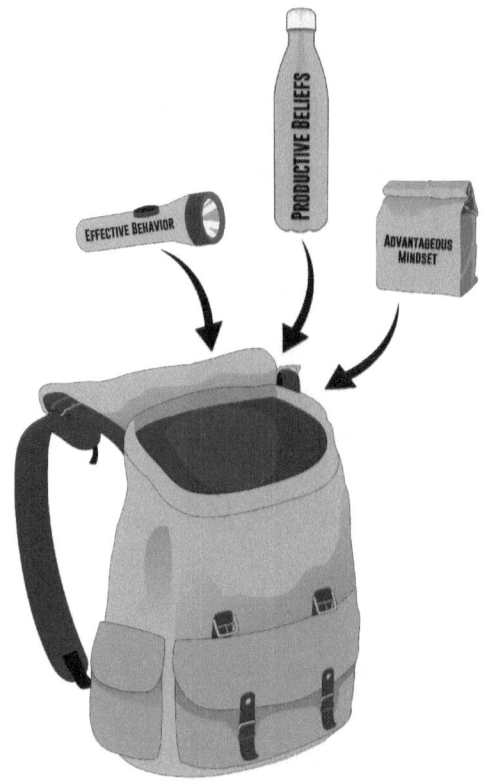

Remember, productive beliefs are not just concerned with your higher beliefs, such as your faith, life philosophy, and so forth. Productive beliefs are more focused on your operational beliefs, the mental software that informs your behavior according to your idea of survival and happiness. Productive beliefs are where your higher beliefs and your operational beliefs align.

The struggle between your higher beliefs and your operational beliefs is the inner battlefield of what Christians understand as the struggle between our spirit and our flesh (Romans 7:23–25). For us, then, it is particularly important that we submit to God's work in us to develop operational beliefs that are not according to fleshly perception, but to the wisdom of His Holy Spirit.

Your submission to Him, which is manifested in your mindset, will facilitate His sanctification of your mind. Believers who display to God the posture of *I get to* are the ones who will experience this transformation of their minds. They continue to show obedience in the *have to* matters of their lives, and they retain their convictions related to their *ought to* issues. But success comes in the *get to* posture. Falling short of that will hinder the growth Christ has planned for you.

Productive beliefs and an advantageous mindset combine to produce effective behavior. These three parts of a life directed by the Holy Spirit will yield godly wisdom, and the place where all three intersect is where strategy is found.

With productive beliefs, an advantageous mindset, and effective behavior in your pack, you are ready to view your relationships strategically, which is a function of godly wisdom. Now you are ready for your new journey. You will hike prepared into your relationships with the sole intention of doing good—engaging them as Christ would.

There is a significant hill you will need to climb before you can learn and implement the influence skills we will show you beginning with the next chapter, even if you already tend to be a strategic individual. You have important relationships to protect. This hill is your existing pressure–management strategy. You must identify it and make a critical change if you have not enjoyed much success up to this point with how you have managed your pressures and stress. You will need to switch from a reactive strategy to a responsive one (see chapter 4).

The hill you must climb comprises three sections:

- Your pressures
- Your pressure–management strategy
- Your stress wounds

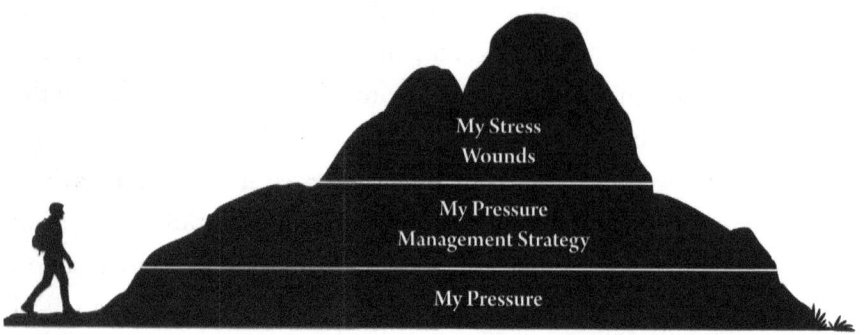

You must examine these parts of your approach to life and relationships and adjust them, if necessary, to be effective with others.

MY PRESSURES

To identify your pressures is not as much about individual pressuring events as it is about learning the *types of pressures* that most cause you the pain of mismanaged stress. Not every pressure has an equal effect on you, and some cause you more discomfort and anxiety than others.

Your task in climbing the first section of your hill is to assess your pressures with these criteria:

- What
- Who
- How much

WHAT

Define your pressures specifically. Don't describe them as symptoms. Being depressed, having a hectic life or hating your job are symptoms of how you manage pressures. Look behind the symptoms and analyze the causes of why you feel the way you do.

Ask yourself these questions:

- What is the exact nature of my pressure?
- What is useful information about my pressure?
- What internal pressure have I created that adds to my stress?
- What parts of my pressure can I control?
- What triggers me to react emotionally to the pressure rather than stay faithful to my strategy?
- What steps can I take to address the part of the pressure that I can control and manage the parts that I cannot?
- What sources of help should I pursue to assist me with this pressure?

WHO

If you aren't sure what your pressures are exactly, it might help to identify where they are coming from. Locate what relationship group is the source of your pressure, including the relationship you have with yourself. This is not a blame game! Don't fall into that trap. We aren't going to blame someone else for your problems and stress. That runs counter to what we believe the Scripture teaches.

Your pressure might come from circumstances that affect the other person, or they may be the result of the choices the other person makes. Either way, you are affected. You can blame the other person, but ultimately, does that remove the pressure? Does that build the relationship? We do not believe that it will.

It is important to identify the relationship group where your pressure is located, however, so you can create strategies appropriate to the individuals involved. In this way, you are putting yourself on the path to respond to your pressures rather than react to them. When you know what your pressure is and where it comes from, there is less chance it will cause you significant pain later on.

HOW MUCH

This is a reverse analysis of your pressure to the one above. Now you want to see how your pressures are affecting others. Looking at pressure and stress this way will indicate which relationships need repair or which ones need a more robust maintenance strategy.

The what–who–how much analysis of your pressures might be a simple approach, but we believe it will take some work for you to become accustomed to looking beyond your symptoms and emotions and learning how to identify your actual pressures. Learning to identify your pressures accurately will lead to the powerful benefit of clarity.

MY PRESSURE–MANAGEMENT STRATEGY

After learning the skill of diagnosing your pressures, you will then be ready to assess something more important, which is how you manage those pressures and the stress that results.

To help you discern whether you have a reactive pressure–management strategy, we showed you five general expressions of reaction in chapter 5, which are:

- Avoidance
- Deflection

- Blame
- Resentment
- Frustration

Each of these expressions are emotion–driven strategies designed by your operational beliefs to alleviate pressure from you. Notice that they are self-focused, do not take into consideration the needs of others (even though you care about them), and they do not reflect the way Christ modeled pressure and relationship management.

If one or more of these are consistent descriptions of your behavior, then you have a reactive approach to pressure management. Ask yourself these questions:

- When a problem or challenge confronts me, do I confront it back with a strategic and proactive approach, or do I let the issue fester and cause me more misery?
- Do I take responsibility for my own actions without excuses or passing my guilt onto others?
- Do I take responsibility for my actions without blaming circumstances or other people? Even if something that affected my behavior was beyond my control, do I own what I do?
- Do I have a resentful spirit?
- What role do exasperated emotions have in my daily reactions to various pressures?

The more you investigate the reasons for your expression of reactive strategy, the better chance you stand of discovering your operating beliefs and why they bring about negative results most of the time. The more important consideration, however, is developing operating beliefs that align with what God desires. Responsive strategy will help you do that.

MY STRESS WOUNDS

The third part of your hill to climb deals with the wounds you have received from prolonged periods of continuous insult of pressure to your emotional well-being. In other words, you need to discover if you have relational stress fractures (chapters 6 and 7).

In chapter 6, we asked you to reflect on whether you could see evidence of emotional damage in yourself. This damage comes in the form of relational stress fractures. Remember, God placed us in relationships with other people and desires that we reflect His attributes to them. We are in those relationships to build up, not tear down.

Review the types of stress fractures listed in the chapter. Do you feel you might have some of these vulnerable places in your emotions where small amounts of pressure can trigger you to exhibit behaviors that contrast with ones God expects of you? These are stress fractures, wounds from the continuous insult of pressure on a part of your life that has grown weak because of the internal pressure you have added from your reactive management strategy.

It is important to know your fractures, if you have any, for two reasons:

First, knowing your stress fractures not only shows you how your emotion–based pressure–management strategy affects you, but it also indicates how you might be affecting others. In chapter 7, you learned about stress concentration. You borrow emotional energy reserved for your relationships to fight against your pressure. That causes you to project your stress onto them, which adds pressure to them. That is not a sustainable strategy.

Ask yourself:

- What are my relational stress fractures?
  - Anger
  - Bitterness
  - Anxiety
  - Money
  - Sex
  - Shame
  - Grief
  - Despair
  - Loneliness
  - Pridefulness
  - Fear
  - Envy
- How might I be adding pressure to others?

Chances are good you will discover ways you are adding the pain of unwanted pressure to those who are important to you, without ever realizing it before.

Second, it is important to identify your fractures because it is critical to understand that they need not be permanent. They can heal. The incremental victories you will experience with a responsive pressure–management strategy will strengthen your beliefs in yourself and in God.

Each success, however small or large, will give you confidence that will enable you to grow stronger and be more effective with your people. Self-knowledge can be painful to gain, but it is very worth it when you do and take the steps necessary to become better.

THE PATH TO EFFECTIVENESS

We titled the chapters in this book in the form of questions because we want you to become accustomed to asking exploratory questions of yourself. Therefore, let's look at our hill again and place our questions at the appropriate places in the graphic.

Don't worry that this will be a very difficult, long climb. It is a hill, not a mountain. Nevertheless, it will be challenging. Make it an optimistic challenge. Remember, you *get to*. Keep in mind the end result, that you will become a person who understands a better way to manage pressure and approach your problems or opportunities strategically, not emotionally.

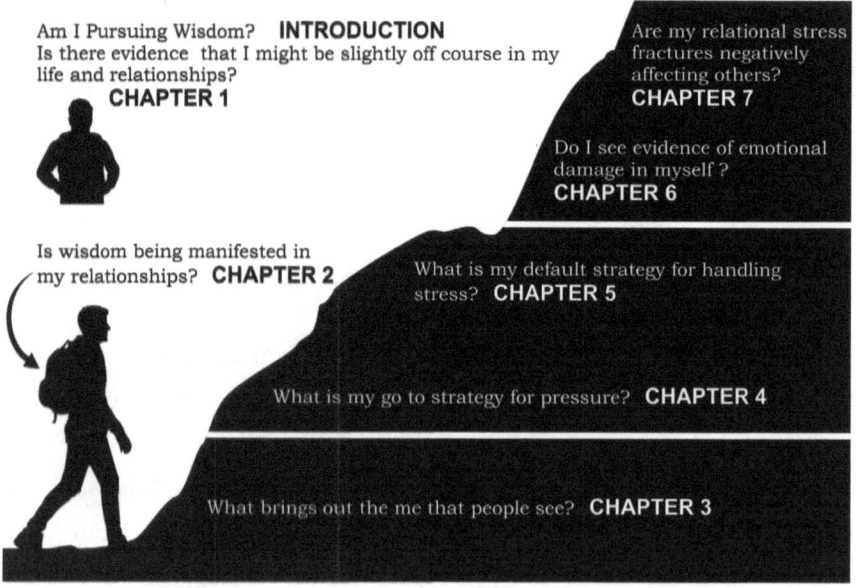

Remember also that there is nothing wrong with emotions if we learn to express them appropriately. God made us emotional creatures. It is just that emotions do not form the basis of an effective pressure–management strategy.

Commit yourself to this effort, because you will need the change in perspective to influence your relationships productively. You don't need a long spiritual retreat to figure this out. God has given you the tools to be spiritually successful. Just ask yourself these questions, and as you come to terms with this new way of thinking, you will be headed onto the path of more meaningful relationships, the kind that accomplishes God's will for you.

Now ask the question from Chapter 8: *What if I could manage my relationships differently?* The answer is you can. It is critical that you do. You have the opportunity and responsibility to benefit the welfare of others.

Now get ready to learn about influence. What is it? Can I be influential? How do I start? These questions will be answered in the remaining chapters. We will discuss civility next. Civility is where influence begins.

10

HOW CAN I STRENGTHEN MY RELATIONSHIPS?

Begin with Civility

If possible, so far as it depends on you, be at peace with all men.
(Romans 12:18)

To begin our discussion of civility, let's consider a story from the Bible that very much reflects its importance. We will look at a remarkable event in the life of one of history's most famous people and how civility both was and was not expressed by the characters involved. From this story, you will learn what it actually means to be civil and how it is possible to express incivility from time to time without realizing it. We will also give you some guiding principles to help you understand how to express civility authentically and consistently.

The term *civility* might not be familiar with younger individuals. It refers to how we should act in society. Humans organize themselves in civilization and are expected to behave differently from animals, who bark, growl, chase, and eat each other. We are higher creatures and are expected to act differently. We often don't, unfortunately. We are sinners, but God requires of us a greater standard of conduct. We are to begin our practice of manners and politeness—civility—in our relationships.

The Bible story regarding civility involves the future King David, when he was hiding from the present King Saul, who was seeking to kill him from a spirit of jealousy. The account is found in 1 Samuel 25:2–38. The following is a summary of what happened.

David was in the territory of Carmel with his 600 loyal warriors. He found out that a wealthy man named Nabal lived in the area and was in a close–by location shearing his sheep. In those days, sheep shearing time concluded with a period of celebration and hospitality. Understanding this, David sent messengers to Nabal asking for some food.

His request was not only based on the custom of hospitality during the celebration but also on the fact that his men were providing protection to Nabal's shepherds while dwelling in the area. The messengers explained this when making their request. They expected that Nabal would show appreciation for their kindness to his shepherds, as well as generosity in celebration of God's provision. He didn't.

He replied with hostility, questioning David's importance and motives for leaving Saul's service. He was absolutely rude and uncaring to the men and was indifferent to David's needs. When the messengers returned to tell David how Nabal replied, he was furious. He ordered 400 of his men to put on their swords with the intention of going to Nabal's estate and killing him and the men of his household.

Meanwhile, one of Nabal's servants went to his wife, Abigail, and informed her of the incident. Abigail was horrified at her husband's behavior and immediately gathered up a large portion of food and beverage for David and his men. She hurried to him with her gift and calmed him with her gracious spirit, agreeing that her husband was indeed foolish, as indicated by the meaning of his name.

David was moved by Abigail's kindness and generosity. He even credited her with saving him from committing bloodshed, which he was about to do. He accepted her gift and sent her home in peace. When Nabal woke up from his drunken sleep from the party he threw the night before, Abigail told him about her encounter with David.

It is certain she let him know how close he was to being slaughtered in retribution for his terrible behavior toward the future king. The news shocked him so much that he suffered what appears to be a stroke. The attack left him completely immobile. Ten days later he died.

If you were asked who in the story lacked civility, who would you say it was? Nabal, right? Absolutely. He was, judging by the Bible's description of him, a pig of a man. His incivility remains legendary.

David was right to be angry, wasn't he? It was the insult to his pride and honor that boiled his blood that day. His cause was righteous, but Nabal scorned what he stood for, dismissing him as a runaway servant with ignoble motives. Who wouldn't be outraged over such treatment?

David's emotions were understandable, if not justified, but what about his reaction? He heard Nabal's reply from the mouths of his own messengers and flew into a rage. He fully planned to lead 400 men to Nabal's location and wipe him out. Who was he to speak so harshly about him, calling into question his motives? Nothing seems to insult people more than accusing them of motives they do not have.

David was about to step on the warpath. Left unchecked, he would have killed who knows how many people innocent of wrongdoing against him. He would have left Nabal's shearing place as bloody as the battlefields where he fought against Philistine warriors. Part of his legacy would have been deadly revenge.

We ask you again, who was being uncivil in this story?

Nabal was, for sure. But so was David. We tend to think being uncivil is on the part of the instigator. However, it can also be on the part of the one being "victimized" by that incivility. As David showed, uncivil reactions often are worse than the uncivil actions that provoked them.

Which was worse? A loud, stingy, rude blowhard's ugly comments, or a field full of murdered people?

There is a mystifying psychological depth to the part of our pride that gets so offended when others question or express doubt in our honor and intentions. We are generally quicker to forgive someone who damages our property or shows negligence in matters that affect us than we are to those who insult our pride. We rage against any insinuation that we are less than we believe ourselves to be. We call it pridefulness. The Bible would label it as the sinful nature of our flesh, as Solomon wrote, "Every man's way is right in his own eyes, but the LORD weighs the hearts" (Proverbs 21:2).

Is it any wonder that relationships suffer damage as much as they do? Even in the most solid households, churches, workplaces, and friendships can relationships be vulnerable to incivility. Incivility can come in many expressions:

- Passive–aggressive hostility
- Shouting
- Manipulative tears
- Pouting
- Arguing
- Emotional isolation
- Inauthentic spiritual rebuke
- Grudges
- Tantrums
- Insults
- Self-righteous responses (taking the "high road")

These are just a few. They come so naturally because being reactive is an instinctive default setting. Nevertheless, relationships suffer insult each time we employ uncivil words and behavior to defend our pride from the other person.

How can we protect ourselves and others from the invisible emotional savagery that comes with incivility? Here are four guiding principles:

STAY IN YOUR GET TO MINDSET.

We know we have talked about this quite a bit, but we want you to see how relevant it is to all parts of human relations to have a *get to* perspective. Remember, *get to* is the mindset of opportunity. *Have to* and *ought to* are the mindsets of obligation. Projecting obligation onto your people decreases the value they believe you see in contributing to their best interests.

Think about these scenarios:

- How would your spouse feel if they knew that you felt you *ought to* work toward having a stable marriage?
- What does it communicate to your boss about your attitude and reliability when you express a mindset that you *have to* come to work every day?
- Do you think your children or grandchildren don't notice your posture of obligation, of *having to* attend their events?
- What do you communicate to your church leadership when you come to church "obediently" to God each week because you feel you should? What does that say to God, for that matter?

Relationships respond to optimism. The other person may not be optimistic or respond to the optimism you express, but your relationship with that person will be blessed by your *get to* spirit.

The foremost benefit is that your pursuit of the best possible outcome will make you less likely to respond with incivility when conflict or hostility arises.

Aspirational people tend to be optimistic because it makes positive outcomes more likely.

THINK IN TERMS OF EFFECTIVE VS. INEFFECTIVE.

95FIVE believes that thinking this way is a brilliant approach to life and relationships. That is why we use that frame of reference in this book. There is moral vs. immoral and right vs. wrong, of course. We should maintain our principles and convictions and strive for behavior that aligns with our moral principles.

Morality comes into relationships, for sure. However, on the practical side of our behavior, morality and ethics express themselves in terms of effectiveness or ineffectiveness, especially in relationships.

God didn't just make up random rules that we would have to abide by to please Him. He gave His law and revealed His standards because moral behavior is effective behavior.

Living ethically and righteously brings about the best outcomes. The way you treat your people is a moral issue, but that is because it is an effective issue.

Again, don't put aside your moral standards, but begin viewing them in light of outcomes and results. When you do that, your perspective shifts to a more holistic view of your performance in your relationships. Is the way you treat your friends effective? How about your in-laws? Do you pursue positive results from the way you relate to the vendor who comes into your office each week? Are you being effective in that business relationship?

Here are two questions you can ask yourself when it comes to effectiveness in your relationships:

I CAN, BUT SHOULD I?

No, you cannot do anything you want to do, but there are many things you can do that might not be very effective. The apostle Paul said to the Corinthian church, "All things are lawful, but not all things are profitable. All things are lawful, but not all things edify. Let no one seek his own good, but that of his neighbor" (1 Corinthians 10:23–24).

Those are great relationship verses, written in the context of eating food in public that may have been first sacrificed to idols, a common practice of paganism. Eating such food will not harm you, but if someone perceives the food as polluted, we should not eat it to protect the sensitivity and conscience of the other person. Was the apostle speaking in terms of morality? Absolutely. But he was also speaking in terms of effectiveness.

You build the other person up by being effective in your own behavior.

- You can rebuke someone for negligence, but should you? Perhaps in some cases you can. But in a particular situation, should you? Maybe taking a different approach is what that person will best respond to.
- You can complain to human resources that a supervisor disrespected you. But should you? Again, in some situations maybe. But what about your witness to that supervisor? Maybe the disrespect was unintentional, or they had pressures they were having trouble managing.
- You can avoid your cousin because of the wrong they did to the family. But should you? How effective would that be to have another marginalized relative seethe in anger and bitterness? Does it bring restoration between them and the others? Not at all.

Some things you can do, and maybe even have the right to do, but how far are you willing to go to be an agent of peace and edification to others?

IS GOD HONORED BY MY DOCTRINAL INTEGRITY WITHOUT INTENTIONAL RELATIONSHIP INTEGRITY?

Lack of civility often comes from people who feel their beliefs are correct, and that any other point of view is errant. Christians especially are vulnerable to this approach, not because they are worse than other people, but because the doctrines of our faith mean so much to us we can't imagine believing anything else.

Because our beliefs are dear to us, people who don't share our convictions are seen as outsiders. If they don't seem to be open to our doctrines, or are Christians who have other doctrines, we view them with suspicion and in many cases are unwelcoming to them altogether. We fear corruption from the world to the extent that we take a fortress approach to our lives and faith.

This is not to say that doctrinal distinctions within the body of Christ at large are not important. They are. Nor should we let our guard down and let ungodly forces infiltrate our spiritual families. However, how do we honor the Lord if we only hold on to our beliefs but not to the precious nature of our relationships? Is it effective to do so?

We were placed here in this life to build up others by reflecting God's attributes to each other. How can we pray for mission opportunities around the world if we aren't willing to be missionaries in our relationships? Yes, they are always there. They test our patience. They are challenging and at times they bug us. But God gave them to us. Learning to be effective in relationships is, we believe, the highest expression of faithful service to the Lord.

ASK WHAT IS MORE IMPORTANT, WINNING THE BATTLES OR STRATEGIZING FOR THE BIGGER PICTURE?

Relationships shouldn't be battlefields, but combat is a frequent occurrence. Incivility, in all of its expressions, pits us against each other. Some people are so bent on winning every argument and having every last word that they do far more destruction to the relationship by winning individual battles than taking the longer view.

There should be a bigger frame of reference in your relationships. You can't determine how other people choose to view them, but you know they are a long–term campaign. Your strategy might need to be flexible and forgiving, putting aside your pride once in a while to not be seen as the victor. You don't need to be wrong, but you don't need to always "win" either.

Have you ever heard the term *pyrrhic victory*? It is winning a battle at such a great cost that the effort wasn't worth it. You lose more than you gain, effectively experiencing defeat as much as your opponent. Individuals who have to overcome everyone else all the time are ones not in the correct frame of mind to be effective in relationships.

DETERMINE WHETHER YOU WOULD HAVE FAIRNESS OR FREEDOM.

Life is not fair, but we sure try to make it that way, particularly for ourselves. We demand justice in every aspect of our human experience in society, particularly our relationships. People of faith look to God to enact justice so that we can avoid unfair treatment. And that, we believe, is a problem.

Stand up for human rights and civil rights where you are able to do so. But reconsider the concept of fairness in your relationships. That will never be a guaranteed benefit. Other people will not always be fair to you, nor will you be to them.

We get so blinded by our egos that we complain about how much the other person refuses to respect our dignity. They insult us with the way they communicate with us or treat us. We elevate our expectations of them to perform in the way that suits our emotional well-being or helps to maintain our self-esteem.

Remember David's experience? Was he treated fairly by Nabal? Not at all. But David expected to be treated differently, and his retribution against

Nabal would have created a lot of widows and fatherless children. Would that have been just?

Here is a critical reality we must come to grips with: as long as you cling to what you believe is fair, you will never be free. Your body and mind might be free, but not your emotions. Not your spirit.

People who insist on fairness will by default be defensive. Defensiveness leads to reactiveness. Reactiveness is an emotion–driven pressure–management strategy. Applying such a pressure–management strategy to your relationships will create the same kind of relationship strategy. What are the fruits of an emotion–driven relationship strategy? Incivility. If you relate to other people only based on your feelings, your perception will be distorted and eventually you will have episodes where you lack civility when healing is needed.

Practicing civility is difficult when the other person refuses to acknowledge or is ignorant of the fact that they are being uncivil. It is a skill and mindset that we do not develop easily, but it is crucial that we continue to work at it, for our sake and for those of our relationships.

LEARNING CIVILITY

Now that we have seen how to avoid incivility, we want to know how to practice civility. We can look to Nabal's wife, Abigail, to show us. Her example shows us that civility is a skill. It takes a great deal of self-awareness to keep yourself in check to prevent acting out emotionally. You may not always feel civil, but you can practice. Doing so is an example of strategy over feelings.

We see in Abigail's demonstration of civility a strategy that comprises three components. They are:

1. **Peace**
2. **Empathy**
3. **Goodwill**

These may look like typical vague terms used when discussing human relations, but if you see how Abigail used them in managing her pressure, which was to deal with an angry famous war hero and future king, you will understand the brilliance and power of her strategy. These three components of civility are at the heart of influence.

PEACE

Abigail began by acting as an agent of peace. Upon hearing the news of her husband's despicable behavior, she immediately gathered up the necessary food and beverage to satisfy David's needs. Then she went as quickly as she could to where David was located (verses 18–20).

Had she not hurried, it would have been too late. He was already on the way when she found him. When they met, she got off her donkey quickly and bowed in respect for someone of his stature. Then she did something that might not make sense. She placed the blame upon herself.

Why did she do that? Why not apologize for her husband's conduct and go from there? It is because she was using a powerful influence skill. She wasn't being dishonest or self-sacrificing to atone for her unworthy spouse. Those are deceptive and manipulating tactics. Instead, what Abigail did was transfer responsibility to herself.

On a subconscious level, the angry warrior was directed to look to Abigail for an alternative to mass slaughter. Had she begged and pleaded for David's mercy, she would have positioned herself as a desperate person. David would have viewed her as a weak alternative to the impassioned action he was about to undertake. Abigail's desired outcome would have stood a poor chance of being realized.

Instead of reacting, she responded. She presented herself as the one responsible for a solution, and the presence of all the donkeys carrying food resonated with David's heart and confirmed that she was able and prepared to make the situation right. She wasn't reconciling David with Nabal. She was reconciling David with a better approach. She stood in the gap, if you will, between David's wrath and the potential victims who would suffer for the foolishness of their employer.

Consider how you can be an agent of peace in a relationship experiencing conflict or decay. We aren't asking you to martyr yourself and take the blame. Blame, actually, is not in the equation of an effective relationship strategy. It wasn't in Abigail's. She wasn't saying, "Please, David, it was my fault. Don't kill us." Instead, she was the one who opted for the mature approach and said, "Let's look for a solution."

EMPATHY

The second component of Abigail's strategy, which was even more powerful, was empathy. Empathy is the choice of trying to view a situation from the perspective of the other person. Much conflict could be avoided if people would just practice this one thing. Individuals known for their negotiating skills are ones who understand this principle.

Abigail practiced empathy for David's viewpoint. Empathy says, "I want to see it your way. I understand why you are thinking or acting the way you do. It makes sense that you feel the way you do."

Abigail showed empathy to David in two ways:

- She empathized with his feelings
- She empathized with his cause

Emotions should not drive strategy, as we have said, but we ought to empathize with the emotions of the other person. When we understand their feelings more, we can guide them to a more productive outcome. This is what Abigail did.

She said, "Don't pay attention to my worthless husband. He is as foolish as his name implies. I was unaware of the presence of your servant, or the outcome might have been different" (verse 25). That was the gist of her statement, but what she was doing was saying, "I understand why you feel the way you do."

People crave understanding of their feelings, and the cause of a great deal of our own frustration is the lack of understanding from others. We want to be understood. When someone sees a matter from your point of view, they are coming to your side. They may not approve of what you are doing, but they do position themselves as your advocate. It is difficult to describe just how important empathy is.

Not only did she empathize with David's feelings, but Abigail also empathized with his cause. She knew who he was and why he was dwelling in the wilderness. He wasn't a worthless servant of the king running away from his duties for suspicious reasons, as Nabal suggested. Therefore, she spoke of the promise of God to give David a strong reign and that David was "fighting the battles of the Lord" (verse 28).

When you can show another person that you understand their point of view, you will go a long way toward influence. You practice civility with the skill of empathy. You aren't saying, "I know how you feel" but "I understand why you feel." The first statement is seldom true. The second statement is authentic and communicates understanding.

GOODWILL

This component is even more powerful than the first two, because it completes the aim of true influence. It is the most civil behavior we can express. Abigail displayed goodwill to David.

Goodwill doesn't just signify the act of being nice or gracious. The way we understand it in the realm of relationship influence is the act of promoting the best interests of the other person. That doesn't mean neglecting your own interests, but making sure you are interested in the well-being of the other person. Abigail did this brilliantly.

While empathizing with the perspective of David, she insinuated that not taking revenge was important in realizing the blessings and promises of God (verses 26–28). But her concluding statement was where her goodwill was especially effective. She said, "When the LORD has fulfilled for my lord [David] every good thing he promised concerning him and has appointed him ruler over Israel, my lord will not have on his conscience the staggering burden of needless bloodshed or of having avenged himself" (verses 30–31 NIV).

Abigail was looking out for the welfare of the future king. Yes, she wanted to avoid wholesale slaughter in her own household, but because of her overtures of peace and her practice of empathy, her desire for the best outcome for David was received as genuine and sincere. She looked after David's conscience, his legacy, and his soul. Her goodwill turned his heart.

YOU AND CIVILITY

The brilliance of the skill of civility lies in its simplicity. Civility recognizes the psychological needs of others. It is not manipulative. Rather, it seeks to communicate to individuals that they are of worth, and their viewpoint has validity. None of us like being dismissed with accusations of motives that we do not have. We do not cope well with wounded pride.

Abigail showed us the way to be civil, and to lessen the chances of conflict to escalate to the point where significant damage is done to our relationship. She was a true diplomat of the side of goodness. As such, she was very effective.

Can you be as well? Without a doubt, you can and will. Just make Abigail's three civility skills a part of your relationship strategies.

1. **Be an agent of peace.** If conflict is necessary, do your part to channel it productively. Don't cause damage to the relationship. Seek to find points of reconciliation and do what you can to meet the needs of the other person.

2. **Practice empathy.** This is a must. If you don't, you are only seeking your own interests. That communicates a profound lack of care and understanding for the other person, and they will respond to you with that same lack of empathy.

3. **Pursue the best possible outcome, which involves seeking the best interests of the other person.** When we see with clarity the possible outcomes of our intentions, we tend to make the best choice. When the other person sees you are on their side as well as your own, you will make better progress toward a healthier relationship.

How can you strengthen your relationships? Begin with civility. Again, that is where influence begins. We will continue our look at influence in the next chapter as we discuss what is involved in our thinking process. You will learn about how your beliefs and perception work together to influence your behavior.

11

WHAT IS BEHIND HOW I MANAGE MY PRESSURE AND RELATIONSHIPS?

Beliefs, Perception, and Behavior: Your Inner Map of Reality

For everyone who partakes only of milk is unacquainted with the word of righteousness, for he is an infant. But solid food is for the mature, who because of practice have their senses trained to distinguish between good and evil.
(Hebrews 5:13–14)

We began with a study on civility in the last chapter to start off the section of this book that focuses on influence. Influence begins with civility. In fact, civility is the face of influence.

You can act civil, however, and not be influential in a way that builds quality relationships. Manners can camouflage hostility. True civility, though, is empty of hostility. There may be episodes of conflict, even in a healthy relationship, but there need not be hostility. Conflict without hostility is not a natural response, but it can be a useful skill for you.

What separates genuine civility from the kind that is self-serving? Our beliefs and perception. In this chapter, you will learn about how these two familiar terms inform how we think and act in light of our influence with others. Your beliefs and perception write your inner map of reality.

BELIEFS

We have already mentioned the importance of your beliefs, using the categories of higher beliefs and operational beliefs. Your operational beliefs are the invisible programming in your mind concerned with your survival. These often override your higher beliefs because your perceived survival or happiness is at stake, at least according to your subconscious.

Operational beliefs are mostly useful. If you have any common sense, it would be found there. Your instincts and intuition—your gut feelings— are as well. They cause you to make choices such as:

- Not going into a fenced–in area that has a threatening– looking dog in it
- Staying in touch with our extended family
- Buying a cold drink at the drive-through on a hot day
- Paying your utility bills so your family can live comfortably
- Defending your loved ones against the attacks of critics or adversaries

They also work against you if you aren't careful. They might motivate you to:

- Spend too much money on a new car because it has more features than the one you can afford
- Misrepresent your role on the project team to ensure job security
- Refuse your relative the benefit of the doubt when accusations start swirling around in the family network
- Go from church to church, never being satisfied with any congregation

What you do and think in your everyday affairs are products of your operational beliefs. You might ask, "If my operational beliefs often contradict my higher beliefs, does it mean my faith and view of reality are not solid parts of my belief system?" The answer is, not at all!

Let's look at your higher beliefs for a moment. 95FIVE views them in three categories:

1. **Your worldview**
2. **Your philosophy**
3. **Your values**

WORLDVIEW

For the purposes of categorizing beliefs, 95FIVE defines worldview as your belief about the origins of everything. Regardless of your religion, or lack of religious conviction, you have your belief about how the universe came about and how it operates. If a person doesn't know or care, that is a worldview as well.

PHILOSOPHY

Admittedly, this may not be a welcome word to everyone, as it reminds us of the academic deep thinkers who write their systems of thought in jargon most of us have difficulty understanding. But we use this word, because each of us essentially do in our hearts what the professional philosophers do on paper or in university classrooms. We develop a way of viewing the world that we feel aligns with our worldview. We observe society and make deductions based on what is in our worldview. This is our personal philosophy. It includes matters such as:

- Our political preferences
- Our opinions of social issues
- Our outlook on the future of civilization, or the importance of history
- Our opinions on the importance of social traditions or developments, such as sports or technology

A person's life philosophy is rarely, if ever, set in stone.

New information, deeper insight, intellectual growth, and maturity are contributing factors that better align our life philosophy with our worldview.

Your life philosophy will only appear finalized once and for all if you resist these growth factors. You will make yourself a victim of the notion that because your worldview is unchangeable, so must your philosophy be, too.

VALUES

Your values are the more practical area of your beliefs. We categorize them into:

1. **Your essentials**
2. **Your principles**
3. **Your code**

ESSENTIALS

Essentials are the parts of life we regard the most. It is hard to imagine the world, or our lives in particular, without them. They are our hobbies, our tastes, our aspirations for society, even our traditions. They hold varying degrees of importance, but they are what gives our lives beauty and meaning. Essentials are admittedly a broad range of what we define as important, but they represent the pleasure and satisfaction we get out of our lives. They include things such as:

- Classic cars
- The holiday season and its traditions

- Gardening
- Travel
- Learning
- Living in the country or in a city
- Community
- Sports
- Outdoor recreation

Why is it important to recognize our own essentials? It is because they are a significant part of our definition of happiness, which informs our operational beliefs to influence many of the decisions we make. Essentials go beyond emotional needs. They are part of your idea of what makes life worthwhile. Some of them tend to change after a while. Others remain with us.

PRINCIPLES

Your principles are your rules to live by. There are many timeless principles that we learn, such as the Golden Rule: "Do unto others as you would have them do unto you." Jesus said that, and a variation of this rule exists in nearly every traditional ethical system throughout history.

You have principles those who raised you taught you (i.e., it is impolite to talk with your mouth full) and by the many teachers throughout your education. The Bible is filled with principles that teach us how to live and think. We even develop some of our own based on what we observe and learn. Principles are often passed down to younger generations in the hopes that our kids will live by them and be successful in life.

CODE

People often label this part of their belief structure as their code of conduct. It is the way they decide ahead of time how they will act in future situations. Our code is generally tied to our principles, but it is important to understand the distinction between the two.

For example, you might embrace a principle that says, "Do not align yourself with foolish people." You might then have a corresponding code that says, "I won't put up with nonsense." The principle is the rule. The code is your definition of how you will live according to that rule.

Unfortunately, it is common to have contradictory codes. Many people embrace the principle of Jesus that says, "Love your enemies and pray for those who persecute you, so that you may prove yourselves to be sons of your Father who is in heaven" (Matthew 5:44–45). How many of them, though, have as part of their code the determination that "I won't be a doormat to anyone. If they attack me, I will give it right back. God doesn't want pushovers serving Him."

A good exercise would be to review how your personal code compares with the principles you say you embrace. When it comes to matters of "survival," those in the example above will behave from operational beliefs that will align with their code rather than with their principle. Your values say a lot about your approach to life and relationships.

SURVIVAL AND HAPPINESS

Your operational beliefs are concerned with your sense of survival and your pursuit of happiness. You want the pleasure of satisfactory relationships and the experiences that help you enjoy life. Your operational belief function will drive you to make choices that ensure your idea of happiness.

You also don't want to be subject to any pressure forces that threaten your idea of what it means to survive. Survival, in this sense, doesn't just refer to literal life or death outcomes, but to efforts to preserve your position in a group or to maintain your dignity. The typical human notion of survival includes saving our jobs or getting ahead in our finances, or many of the other priorities we feel help us make it in society.

Make no mistake, survival is important. Stewardship and aspiration should be integral to our drive to maintain and grow our influence.

However, our operational beliefs become counterproductive when survival degenerates into conquest and happiness into gratification.

If your idea of survival means stepping on people to get what you want, then your survival definition is corrupted. The same goes for happiness. If your pursuit of happiness is indulgence in gratifying activities, you need a renewal of your idea of what it means to be happy.

This brings us back to the question of why our operational beliefs often contradict our higher beliefs. Survival and happiness are the determining factors. We choose, mostly on the subconscious level, according to what secures these two basic human drives.

Earlier, you learned that our Christian view of "the flesh" is centered on our operational beliefs. It is important to know that our flesh—not our literal skin and muscle tissue, but our natural drive to survive and be happy—is not the same thing as our old nature. Our old nature, what we were before our salvation in Christ, was an incurable disposition to view reality with ourselves as our sole reference point, making us self-centered by default.

We had no other choice. We did not yet receive the miracle of God's transforming work in us. Even though many people know of God, they don't know Him. In other words, there is no relationship with their creator. A person with a new nature in Christ can sit next to an unredeemed person with their original nature in the same church service, worshipping the same God, but with two entirely different understandings of who He is and what He is about.

That is the old nature. It existed in deception until Christ shined His light into us (2 Corinthians 4:3–6) and made us into new creatures (2 Corinthians 5:17). We are helpless to change our natures. It must be an act of God (Romans 5:6–8).

Our flesh is not the same thing as our old nature, even though the two were often viewed in Scripture together (Romans 8:5–8). Our old natures are dead (powerless), but we still live in bodies with minds that our old sin nature has affected. Our flesh reflects our old natures because it was ruled by them until Christ saved us. Now we have new natures, but we still have the presence of our fleshly minds that have been conditioned by our previous self-centered approach to managing our lives.

Our responsibility as believers is to live according to our new natures, which desire to do the will of God. If we do not, then we live according to our flesh, which reflects the sinful pride of our old natures. Doing so will contradict our new natures and bring misery, conviction, and even God's disciplinary intervention.

Letting our operational beliefs determine our behavior according to the corrupt sensibilities of our flesh amounts to living like an unregenerate person even though God gave us the gift of a new nature. Living according to our flesh doesn't always mean going out and committing serious sins. Where our flesh does its most effective work is when it mingles its version of our operating beliefs with our higher beliefs, specifically our values.

This manifests in behavior such as:

- I will stand for what I believe is true, even if it hurts other people.
- It isn't right to let others get away with faulty arguments or wrong opinions.
- We have to get rid of the pastor. Our church is shrinking.
- If you aren't strict with your kids, they will never learn.
- The boss might take advantage of other employees, but not me.
- My spouse will not speak to me that way. I won't tolerate it.

See how these operational beliefs seem founded on what is true or reasonable? However, the relationship strategy implied in these statements suggests a course of action that would not honor God or reflect the new nature He gave you. You can fight for the cause of the Lord, but if you fight for Him with the same methods you used to fight for yourself in your old nature, your flesh is manipulating your operational beliefs. Therefore, how about:

- I will stand for what is true with the goal of helping others understand that truth, even if they never embrace it.
- I will honor the right of other people to have their opinions and arguments, even if I don't agree with them. I will make my case as clearly and peacefully as I can.
- Unfortunately, it might be time for our pastor to step away from his ministry here. It could be, however, that the congregation is at fault for our lack of growth. We should pray together and seek what the Holy Spirit wants us to know.
- Being firm with our children is important, as long as we balance our discipline with love and flexibility when appropriate. We want them to learn the right way, not have it forced upon them.
- The boss seems to take advantage of company employees. If that is true, the right thing to do is earn trust, do my best, and build a relationship that seeks everyone's best interest.
- I don't like how my spouse communicates with me lately. Clearly something is wrong and the best thing I can do is model godly and loving communication.

These more effective alternatives reflect the higher beliefs we embrace regarding the principles the Bible teaches us. Our corrupted flesh does not view matters this way. However, we were given the authority and responsibility to turn the reins of our operational beliefs over to our new natures, which in submission to the Holy Spirit can reform the parts of our belief structure that negatively influence the way we behave.

What is the practical way that we can submit to Him for this purpose? By cooperating with Him as He guides our perception.

PERCEPTION

There are two parts of the definition of perception, according to *Merriam-Webster.com Dictionary*, that are helpful to this subject[3]. They are:

1. awareness of the elements of environment through physical sensation

2. a capacity for comprehension

As perceptive beings, we can interact with our environment through our senses of sight, hearing, smell, taste, and touch. We do a lot of learning that way. So do animals. Our creator gave us something greater, however. He gave us the capacity to think and reason about concepts and ideas. We can read, watch, or listen to recorded information, as well as record our own.

This means that God gave us the power of observation and the intellect to make sense of what we experience. This is how we learn and grow. We have a distinctly human perception unlike that of our animal friends. Tragically, though, our distinctively human perception is affected by distinctively human sin.

That makes our flesh what it is, a side of us that is naturally hostile toward God (Romans 8:7). With salvation, our hostile affections are done away with, but sometimes our flesh motivates us to hostile actions. It is a challenging and sometimes aggravating process to resist the operating beliefs of our corrupt flesh and employ those taught by the Spirit of God.

> For I joyfully agree with the law of God in the inner person, but I see a different law in the parts of my body waging war against the law of my mind, and making me a prisoner of the law of sin, the law which is in my body's parts. Wretched man that I am! Who will set me free from the body of this death? (Romans 7:22–24)

---

3   Merriam-Webster.com Dictionary, s.v. "perception," accessed July 19, 2022, https://www.merriam-webster.com/dictionary/perception.

Our bodily appetites call upon our operational beliefs to pursue survival and pleasure, which often is in the form of conquest and gratification.

In the church culture, we often urge each other to just "give it to God" or surrender our desires to Him. "Let go, let God" is another pious recommendation that leaves people scratching their heads and wondering how they are to do that. In our attempts at effective and results–producing surrender to Christ's lordship, we:

- Try to pray more and pray longer
- Strengthen our willpower to be more obedient
- Participate in more religious activity
- Go to retreats and revivals
- Commit to reading large sections of Scripture every day (until we get to Leviticus)
- Indulge in guilt feelings, which makes us feel repentant
- Seek the counsel of other believers, many of whom also do the things on this list

We aren't meaning to be critical here, but there is an avenue to pursue that will help us get better results in our Christian behavior than the above strategies, some of which are good to do, but not in our own strength, which is what often happens. If you want more effective spiritual and behavioral production from prayer, Bible reading, revival attendance, and so forth, then address the issue of your operational beliefs in the area of your perception.

It begins there. Ask God for guidance and wisdom to help you view matters as He does. It is the highest act of empathy you can practice. You learn to see and think the way Christ does. His thoughts and actions are in perfect alignment with the Heavenly Father. They, along with the Holy Spirit, are one. If your perception aligns with Christ, it aligns with God. That is His will.

And do not be conformed to this world, but be transformed by the renewing of your *mind,* so that you may *prove what the will of God is,* that which is good and acceptable and perfect. (Romans 12:2, emphasis added)

Have this *attitude* [*mind* in the King James Version] in yourselves *which was also in Christ Jesus.* (Philippians 2:5, emphasis added)

These are some principles to remember, regarding the sanctification of your perception:

1. Trying to consistently think and behave in ways that contradict your fleshly operating beliefs without trusting in God to help you change your perception is all but futile. Even if you do manage consistency in godly behavior, you have not dealt with your perception and therefore there is a conflict within you. By your own willpower will you persist in correct living, but you will lack the empathy for Christ's viewpoint. Your actions will appear spiritually motivated, but your thinking will remain aligned with your flesh. This will hinder you from going beyond "correct" behavior to think in terms of strategy for your life and relationships.

2. Godly perception feeds your belief structure useful and truthful information, which will align your values with operating beliefs that honor God and build relationships.

3. It takes faith to participate with God's will in this way. So many of us try to "have more faith" without understanding how to do so. Ask God to increase your faith and to give you wisdom (Mark 9:24; James 1:5). He wants you to have it. Only then will you succeed.

Training your perception under God's guidance begins with knowing His word (Psalm 119:1–16). Humbly place yourself under Christ's supervision. Be His disciple (learner). Let His word change your perception so that in your everyday life you will see your relationships as He does.

The next chapter will show you what else is a part of your thinking and behavior, particularly regarding your relationships. Character and pride are an essential part of you, and together they create the person who other people see. Influence begins with civility and is shaped by our beliefs. Character is at the heart of it.

12

HOW AM I VIEWED BY OTHERS?

The True Function of Your
Character and Pride

*In all things show yourself to be an example of good deeds, with
purity in doctrine, dignified, sound in speech which is beyond reproach, so that the opponent will be put to shame, having nothing
bad to say about us.*
(Titus 2:7–8)

In the following pages, you are going to learn about your character and
the role of your pride in the way you think and relate to others. You
know it is important to have good character, but we are going to show
you what kind of character is optimal for influence in your relationships.
We believe it is the type of character that God wants to help you develop
to carry out His mission in your relationships with others.

It is also important to understand the role of perception. We looked at
perception in the previous chapter. It draws conclusions based upon your
interaction with your environment and either affirms or modifies your
beliefs according to those conclusions.

This sounds like a straightforward learning process, and in and of itself it is. However, humans have a feature in their minds called pride. Your pride has an interesting influence on your perception, which can either bless or hinder you substantially. We will discuss this dynamic later in the chapter.

First, let's begin with character. Undoubtedly, you were taught that good character is important. Do what is right, develop good habits, and behave accordingly. This will build character in you, according to the generations that came before us. It is what most of us aim for.

Christians have extra incentive, as our role of persons of faith in this fallen world requires godly character to be integral to our testimonies to others. We study Scripture to learn valuable principles that teach us to live as the Lord directs. It is critical that we do so.

It is also a struggle, isn't it? As discussed in the previous chapter, we must live in these "bodies of death" as the apostle Paul called them. We need His help every day to overcome the desires of our flesh and the reactive strategies we employ to ensure our sense of survival and happiness. Not everything you do in the flesh is evil, of course, but your flesh craves independence from God's rule and from accountability with others.

Our flesh is not relationship oriented, except on a self-focused level. Look how Adam and Eve turned on each other when God found them in a state of sin. The Bible has plenty of examples of relationships breaking down due to the operational beliefs of the flesh. You see examples in your world, and perhaps you have been grieved by how it happens in your own life.

The way to add a lot of effectiveness to your approach to your relationships is to pursue good character, but we believe there is a dimension to effective character that most people are unaware of, causing them to struggle with frustration and to miss the primary goal God has for their Christian journey. 95FIVE believes that without the character skill we are about to show you, God's design for relationships will be very difficult, if not impossible, to realize. This concept goes beyond just having fulfilling relationships with those you care about. It places your role in those relationships at the level of purpose that most reflects that of God Himself.

To discover this vital trait of God's character, we can go right to the Ten Commandments. Understandably, a lot of believers regard this list of God's core laws as very solemn and perhaps a little intimidating. However, within them is a remarkable feature of God that can revolutionize our ministry to those in our lives. It is found in the second commandment: *"You shall not make for yourself an idol, or any likeness of what is in heaven above or on the earth beneath, or in the water under the earth. You shall not worship them nor serve them; for I, the LORD your God, am a jealous God . . ."* (Exodus 20:4–5).

God is a jealous God. You have probably heard that before and understand what He meant by His statement. We have a covenant relationship with Him, which is exclusive. Because Jehovah is the only real God, there is no place in our worship or affections for idols that represent figments of our imagination. It won't be tolerated, to be blunt about it. God is jealous.

God has a right to whatever mindset He wishes, doesn't He? Jealous or not, He is God and we better take our position with Him seriously. Idolatry is no trivial matter!

Is that the complete meaning of this revelation of Himself, however? Look at what He says in the rest of His remarks concerning this commandment: *"I, the LORD your God, am a jealous God, inflicting the punishment of the fathers on the children, on the third and fourth generations of those who hate Me, but showing favor to thousands, to those who love Me and keep My commandments"* (Exodus 20:5–6; see Exodus 34:6–7).

The functions of the creator's jealousy are expressed in two ways:

1. His judgment
2. His favor

Notice that both expressions suggest action, not just emotion. Jealousy, in the way we understand it, is an emotion. With God, however, it manifests in action.

Consider His judgment. He said He would inflict the punishment of the fathers onto the children down to the fourth generation. While this sounds completely unfair, it is necessary to understand what He meant by that. First, He was speaking in a corporate sense. If you have a great-grandparent who did really bad things, God will not punish you for it, even though you might have to live with some of the long–term consequences, if there are any.

However, if you are a member of a generation whose previous generations acted in hostility to God and disregarded His laws, He might bring punishment onto your people in your country or clan in which you would share in the suffering. War, poverty, famine, and economic ruin are some ways nations suffer for the choices of previous generations. God often manifests His judgment in consequences.

Second, there is the insinuation that the third and fourth generations are hostile to the Lord as well. It is not as though they are innocent. A repentant generation can turn away God's wrath that was provoked by previous generations. A generation of people who share in their parents' and grandparents' rebellion will invite God's unpleasant intervention.

The point is that a jealous God actively expresses His judgment. He doesn't sulk. He is always in motion, always engaging, continuously working through history, in your nation, in your city, your church, your family, your life.

God's expressed judgment always has a redemptive end to it.

Most who suffer from it will not embrace the offer of salvation or even discern that it is being offered, but many will. He moves in ways we do not understand within a reality we cannot fully comprehend, as Peter wrote, "The Lord is not slow about His promises, as some count slowness, but is patient toward you, not willing for any to perish, but for all to come to repentance" (2 Peter 3:9).

If God moves redemptively in His expressions of judgment, how much more so in His favor to those who love Him by keeping His commandments? Notice how He does not define our love for Him in emotional terms. Our love for Him, if it is to be authentic, is action. We keep His commandments, as the apostle Paul explains, "So then, my beloved, just as you have always *obeyed*, not as in my presence only, but now much more in my absence, *work out* (not for) your own salvation with fear and trembling; for it is God *who is at work in you, both to desire and to work for His good pleasure*" (Philippians 2:12, emphasis added).

We have active love for God because He has active love for us. His jealousy for us moves Him to repel harmful influences and bless us with the benefits of being His children. It is the powerful dynamic of being in covenant with Him.

Now we come to the question of how we reflect that kind of mindset in our relationships with other people. We don't have God's capability of righteous jealousy; ours is corrupted by sin. However, God models for us a related quality that He applies to His relationship with us. We can use it in our relationship to Him, and to those of the other people in our lives. It is called zeal.

The definition of *zeal* is "eagerness and ardent interest in pursuit of something."[4] Often, we tie zeal to extreme passion, and sometimes it is expressed that way. However, zeal is determination and focus. It bridges emotion and the kind of action that has a purpose.

---

4   Merriam-Webster.com Dictionary, s.v. "zeal," accessed July 19, 2022, https://www.merriam-webster.com/dictionary/zeal.

Look at how it is used in Scripture in reference to God's activity on behalf of His people. Keep in mind, these examples are expressions of His holy jealousy.

As for judgment: *"Then my anger will be spent and I will satisfy My wrath on them, and I will be appeased; then they will know that I, the LORD, have spoken in My zeal, when I have spent My wrath upon them"* (Ezekiel 5:13). God was telling Ezekiel that those left behind in Judah by the Babylonians would receive the punishment for their idolatry and unbelief, an expression of their jealous God's zeal. God did this, not to send His people to destruction, but to stir up in their hardened hearts genuine repentance so that they would return to Him.

In another example, the Lord declared Judah would survive the invasion of the Assyrians, who destroyed the kingdom of Israel in the north. He said, *"For out of Jerusalem a remnant will go, and out of Mount Zion survivors. The zeal of the LORD will perform this"* (Isaiah 37:32). In both judgment and favor, God is zealous for the covenant relationship He has with the children of Abraham.

We also see the zeal of God at work in prophecy. Speaking of the future coming of the Messiah, He said, *"There will be no end to the increase of His government or of peace on the throne of David and over his kingdom, go establish it and to uphold it with justice and righteousness from then on and forevermore. The zeal of the LORD of armies will accomplish this"* (Isaiah 9:7).

The ultimate redemptive act of God that would include people from all races was sending Christ into the world as a sacrifice for our sin and as deliverer of those who would trust in Him. Christ Himself modeled the zeal of the Heavenly Father, including when He cleansed the temple of those doing crooked business in the name of religion. His followers reflected on what King David wrote long ago, that "Zeal for your house will consume me" (John 2:17; see Psalm 69:9 and 119:139). They understood that David's statement about himself was also a prophecy about Jesus.

Jesus modeled for us a zeal for God and a zeal for us. It is with this form of action and focus that we can approach our relationships with a godly perspective. Zeal for your relationships will move you to strategy. Strategy is a product of zeal.

Only with zeal can we be jealous of our people the same way God is. We cannot reflect it entirely, as we aren't on His level. But we can understand the passion and strategy it takes to be a relationship builder. In the ancient Hebrew language of the Old Testament, jealousy and zeal both come from the same root word, *qana*. Both expressions come from the same heart that desires the best possible outcome for a relationship.

Jealousy without zeal is:

- Envy
- Mistrust
- Resentment
- Destructive conflict
- Dishonesty
- Possessiveness

Jealousy with zeal comes from an individual who very much cares about the welfare of the other person and the covenant nature of that relationship. Applying a spirit of zeal to a faltering or already damaged relationship gives it a much better chance of being restored. No strategy is foolproof in this world, though. Human nature is what it is.

Even Jesus lost some relationships, not because it was His fault, but because the operational beliefs of fallen people led them to make tragic choices. We do our best and let the guidance of God lead us. In the end, other people make their choices regardless of what we do. However, we also suffer more loss than we need to because we don't understand zeal.

Character marked by holy zeal is the most effective kind in relationships. The force that most hinders our zeal is pride. The role that pride plays in our thinking often stands in our way of seeing relationships that way God does. As such, our perception is influenced by our flesh and is turned inward. We go back to wanting what is best for ourselves.

Understandably, pride has a bad reputation. It is seen as the bad guy when we consider the many faults of human behavior. However, pride only does what it is designed to do.

What is the function of pride? Consider these sets of statements:

1. You smile and nod in agreement after a discussion with someone who sees the matter as you do.
2. You become angry when the discussion turns into an argument.

1. You look with satisfaction at a project you did well.
2. You get frustrated working on a project and throw something in anger.

1. You tell your child how proud you are of how they acted.
2. You tell your child how disappointed you are in how they acted.

1. You pray silently for God's intervention when conflict in your church heats up.
2. You get up and storm out when conflict in your church heats up.

All eight statements involve your pride. The first statement in each set is a positive expression of pride, while the second statements are negative expressions of that same pride. We all have had both types of experiences many times, and whether we ended up glad or angry, it was because of the function of our pride.

So then, what does pride do? It protects our beliefs. Remember, our beliefs are our inner map of reality. They determine how we view everything, what we value and how we believe we are supposed to behave, whether our actions always align with our principles or not. Our beliefs are everything to us. The job of our pride is to defend those beliefs because we rely on them for our survival and happiness. After all, if we didn't have our pride and our beliefs changed with every stimulus, how functional would we be?

We are glad and excited when circumstances or the behavior of others align with how our beliefs say things should be. We can experience feelings of anger when matters do not go our way. If the actions and words of other people align with our beliefs, we might have feelings of harmony. If they do not, we react with varying degrees of defensiveness, hostility, or anxiety. You can see how your pride has a significant effect on your civility.

We are not doomed to have our emotions be in servitude to our pride in this way, though. In fact, being in that frame of mind is the least effective strategy you can have. You are reactive when you are emotionally ruled by your pride. You are enslaved to yourself.

We have a choice. We can choose to detach our feelings from our pride. It isn't easy. In fact, it may be the most difficult part of learning to influence others. It is necessary, though. Nothing squashes influence as much as behavior negatively affected by offended pride.

How do you detach your feelings from your pride?

- Don't spend your energy fighting against your emotions.
- Know when your perception is negatively influenced by your pride.
- Feed your beliefs with useful information.

EMOTIONS

It might sound like 95FIVE does not value emotions. We have gone to great lengths to explain how emotion–based reactive strategy is inefficient. However, that doesn't mean that we don't see the importance of them. We were created as emotional beings. Even God, in His own way, expresses emotion.

It is natural to feel happy or get down in the dumps once in a while. Anger, fear, and joy are all part of our lives. So is every other emotion.

It is counterproductive to fight against having emotions, particularly when you are under pressure and experiencing stress. That expends energy in a futile strategy. The strength of your operating beliefs, based on your values, and their influence on your perception is too strong for your willpower. Put simply, subconsciously you don't want to give up that emotional state.

Consider that your emotion is not what defines who you are. People judge you by your expressions of your emotions, but the emotion itself is merely a reaction to what either aligns with or contradicts your belief system. Emotional expression might give others an idea of who you are, but they can't get the whole picture because they don't know the value system behind your operational beliefs. You probably aren't aware of it completely, either.

That is why we must be guided by truth, not merely doctrines but the behavior that God says must proceed from those higher beliefs. Two equally devoted Christians who believe the same doctrines can have vastly different emotions and reactions to the same issue. This has been observed in the church countless times over the generations.

If you want to evaluate the role of your emotions in your approach to your life and relationships, ask yourself these two questions:

1. What makes me feel the way I do? It has often been said that it isn't *that* we experience an emotion that is important, but what *causes* it. Look at your general emotional state and the emotions you experience most often. What makes you experience them? When you discover the answer, you will be much closer to understanding what your values actually are, not just what you declare them to be. You might be surprised at how humbling and enlightening this self-assessment is.

2. How do I think and behave in reaction to my emotions? This is the "you" that others see. They witness how you handle pressure. They judge your character on this basis, even though they don't

have the complete picture of who you are. Ask yourself if you are being effective or ineffective with your strategy. When you experience a pressure and your emotion flares up, do you fight the emotion, behave according to it, or determine to implement an effective and truth–based strategy in spite of that emotion?

The Bible has a wonderful statement regarding how to process your emotions, using one emotion as an example: "BE ANGRY, AND YET DO NOT SIN; do not let the sun go down on your anger, and do not give the devil an opportunity" (Ephesians 4:26–27). Be angry, but don't sin in that anger. Be fearful, but don't sin. Be happy, but be careful not to sin in your happiness.

PERCEPTION

Your pride seeks to defend your beliefs because they define for you what reality is. Your pride wants to make sure your inner map maintains its integrity. Otherwise, you would be dysfunctional and unable to survive.

Your perception gives your beliefs information by which they are affirmed or challenged.

Because of our fallen nature, however, our pride tends to involve itself inappropriately in our perception. In its defense of your beliefs, it will bias your perception to view matters according to what you already feel is true. Instead of letting our beliefs withstand challenges from what we see or hear, we assume our beliefs are valid and change our perception accordingly.

We don't do this for everything, obviously, but in matters of truth we are susceptible. We wrongly judge God's motives or those of other people based on our biased perception. We must subordinate our beliefs to God's truth.

A biased perception isn't always bad. It is how we protect ourselves from deception. Unfortunately, it is also how we fall for deception. We buy miracle potions for rapid health benefits or embrace phony teaching to gratify our fleshly aspirations in the spiritual realm. It causes us to not give others the benefit of the doubt or be harsh with them for not having opinions or behavior that align with what we feel is true. We harm our relationships because of biased perception.

Our perception should be biased in favor of biblical truth, but when our behavior does not align with that truth, our perception is more biased in favor of subconscious values that are stronger than those we claim are the most important. This endangers our relationship effectiveness substantially.

USEFUL INFORMATION

To increase the effectiveness of our beliefs and our perception, we must feed our beliefs useful information. Useful information, as we understand it, is that which reflects reality, not theory or someone's agenda. Of course, ultimate useful information comes from Scripture. Saturate yourself with it. Listen to sound teaching that is based on it. Doing this will increasingly enable you to defend yourself from deception and blindness to the realities in your life you might not be aware of yet. This is the function of wisdom.

Character is everything when it comes to relationships. You cannot have influence with poor character unless the other person has poor character as well. Of course, we aren't called to build relationships based on deception, but on truth.

Use your pride to benefit you, not to trip you up. Build your beliefs to align more with truth. Feed them useful information. Learn to perceive issues based on truth, not emotion. Defend what is true and reject falsehood.

Finally, brothers and sisters, whatever is true, whatever is honorable, whatever is right, whatever is pure, whatever is lovely, whatever is commendable, if there is any excellence and if anything worthy of praise, think about these things. As for the things you have learned and received and heard and seen in me, practice these things, and the God of peace will be with you. (Philippians 4:8–9)

It is a given that we don't always think and act according to how we believe. Our operational beliefs contain values we may be unaware of or wish we didn't have. As a result, we express thought and behavior that doesn't align with our truth. Our pride understands that, and in order to defend the integrity of our beliefs, it uses some psychological techniques to give us a sense of stability. We will look at those in the next chapter.

HOW DO I ENSURE INTEGRITY IN MY BELIEFS?

The Faces of Pridefulness and the Process of Change

In view of this I also do my best to maintain a blameless conscience both before God and before other people, always.
(Acts 24:16)

What do people tend to do when they fail, mess up, or do what is wrong? They often:

- Make an excuse
- Blame something or someone else
- Lie
- Apologize
- Get down on themselves
- Pretend it didn't happen
- Downplay its seriousness
- Insinuate that they were victimized

We are an interesting species, aren't we? Our minds have a way of shading reality or branding ourselves to make us appear in a better light. Our pride defends our beliefs and opinions with ferocity, and we create narratives in the hopes of improving our own public relations.

We do what we do for many reasons, but much of our thought and behavior centers on another feature of our mental faculties: our conscience. In this chapter, you will learn about how your conscience affects the way your pride does its job of defending your beliefs. You will see how pride turns to pridefulness in an effort to maintain the integrity of your belief structure when your conscience alerts you to inconsistent behavior.

CONSCIENCE AND PRIDE

An individual's conscience is their awareness of right and wrong and is the mental function by which they judge their own behavior. A conscience serves the morality represented by the belief structure of the mind, and it declares to our inner person whether we have behaved accordingly. If we have, our conscience commends us. If not, it condemns our behavior.

Our pride is aware of this. The difficulty lies in defending our belief system that contains both our standards of morality and our operating beliefs, which move us to violate those standards from time to time. With the "voice" of our conscience present, how does pride defend our beliefs from contradictory behavior that comes from those same beliefs? In other words, how does it declare our beliefs valid when they are the source of behavior that does not align with them?

The answer is that our pride uses some powerful techniques to maintain our sense of alignment with our beliefs. After all, no one wants to embrace their own hypocrisy. Our pride needs to solve the dilemma.

It does so with the following techniques:
- Affirmation
- Self-justification
- Self-condemnation

Everyone has utilized most or all of these at one time or another. Some individuals specialize in them. They are natural byproducts of the negative expressions of our pride. We refer to them as pridefulness. As harmful as they can be, they are merely ways with which pride attempts to maintain belief integrity in the face of conscience.

AFFIRMATION

Affirmation sounds like a good thing, and of course it is. It is how we show approval and support for others. There are many great ways we do this: compliments, shared joy, encouragement, constructive criticism, accountability, kindness, and so forth. It is an act of grace and affection that we express to other people.

Where affirmation becomes harmful is when we engage in the many ways we provide it for ourselves. We do it through our self-talk, or we coax it from other people. Here are a few examples:

- Repeating statements of affirmation based on what we wish were true but without the necessary change in our strategy
- Exaggeration in how we represent ourselves
- Name dropping
- Believing we are more significant to someone than we really are
- Fishing for compliments
- Ending nearly every sentence with phrases such as "Know what I mean?" Or "Right?"
- Always seeking approval and behaving sacrificially to get it
- Crafting a personal narrative that paints you as one who struggles against the odds

There are many other prideful techniques designed to bring affirmation our way, but these are common ones. We all need our heads patted now and then, but engaging in manipulative tactics to pull inauthentic affirmation from others is an exercise in self-deception. We do it sometimes, however, because it helps to reconcile our conscience with our inconsistencies. Self-administered affirmation minimizes our sense of guilt and exaggerates feelings of virtue so that we can maintain our perception of the inner unity of our beliefs.

Ask yourself if there are ways you manipulate people to affirm you. Moreover, consider whether you are attempting to coax it from God. You don't need to try that on Him. Just trust in what He says about His approval of you: *"The steadfast of mind You will keep in perfect peace, because he trusts in You"* (Isaiah 26:3).

SELF-JUSTIFICATION

We do our best to draw from the goodwill of others the affirmation we think we need. We also work our magic to justify ourselves to excuse our failures and wrongdoing. Our conscience desires to bear witness against our behavior but often authentic repentance goes against our need to validate our belief structure. So then, we engage in self-justification.

Self-justification is our attempt to justify, or excuse, our behavior. Just like with affirmation, we are pretty inventive in how we try to cloak ourselves in righteousness. We do things such as:

- Make excuses
- Deflect blame
- Be a victim
- Exaggerate our challenges
- Blame Satan
- Emphasize being "a sinner saved by grace"
- Shrug your behavior off as the product of being "still under construction" by God
- Insinuate that God could have prevented you from acting as you did
- Emphasizing that you didn't mean to or want to engage in such behavior

We don't need to remind God that we are imperfect and struggle against our flesh. We should rely on His grace and take responsibility for our actions before others, particularly the ones affected by our choices. As long as you continue to justify yourself, you won't have much influence with people.

SELF-CONDEMNATION

The opposite of justifying yourself is condemning yourself. Self-justification may be more harmful to others, potentially, but self-condemnation is devastating to you. However, your pride can use this practice to maintain the integrity of your beliefs. If your conscience declares your guilt in such a way that your pride can't justify your guilty behavior, then it will react by influencing you to condemn yourself. The integrity of your beliefs is upheld and you, the guilty one, are thrown under the bus, so to speak. You do it to yourself.

This is a tragic feature of the human soul. We can be so prideful that we value our beliefs more than we do ourselves. "Protect those beliefs at all costs!" is the slogan of a self-condemning mindset.

Doesn't this contradict our drive for survival and happiness? Not unless it is taken to the level of self-harm or destruction. That is the exception, however. In most cases, we believe that this treatment of ourselves is an exercise in accountability. We feel as though we are in agreement with God regarding our guilt. Are we, though?

The Scripture says, "Therefore there is now no condemnation at all for those who are in Christ Jesus. For the law of the Spirit of life in Christ Jesus has set you free from the law of sin and death" (Romans 8:1). The rest of the chapter describes beautifully how we are regarded by our Savior.

He doesn't approve of our ineffective and immoral behavior. Nor will He keep from intervening when needed. But He loves us with a love too deep to comprehend. Seeing us condemn ourselves certainly saddens Him and hinders us from enjoying His presence.

LIBERTY

You can be liberated from the burdens of pridefulness. Start by accepting that you have a conscience and your pride. Be grateful for these useful functions that God gave you. Understand that your flesh by nature corrupts their function, but that you have the tools to overcome pridefulness.

Resist the temptation to give up your struggle and dilute your effective beliefs to ease the strength of your conscience. Rather, hold tight to them and seek to build them, as the psalmist wrote, "So I will keep Your law continually, forever and ever. And I will walk at liberty, for I seek Your precepts" (Psalm 119:44–45).

HOW TO START

Begin with a *get to* mindset. Christianity is so much more vibrant and meaningful when we put aside the obligations of *have to* and *ought to*. Again, we have the obligation to obey Christ's commands, but we should want to obey. We get to be a part of something so great as inclusion in the Bride of Christ.

Second, consider this pursuit of liberty from pridefulness as a strategy. We have written a lot about being strategic in your approach to your other relationships, but you have a relationship with yourself. Be strategic about how you cooperate with the Holy Spirit to improve your life and faith.

YOUR STRATEGY

The objective of your strategy is to identify the ineffective values of your operational beliefs and modify them to align with your higher beliefs, or to get rid of them altogether. Keep in mind, this will take faith, patience, experience, and time. It is not easy. But the more you understand and embrace this pursuit, the better you will become at recognizing ineffective values. It might even be a good idea to engage this personal strategy under the guidance of a mentor or professional counselor, if you feel that is needed.

To guide you in creating your strategy, here are some questions to ask yourself:

WHY DO I MAKE CHOICES THAT CONTRADICT MY FAITH AND BRING CONSEQUENCES THAT DO NOT PLEASE GOD?

In answering this question, you are not looking for the stock reasons, i.e., because I struggle with my flesh, or Satan's temptation is strong. You know those facts already. What you are looking for instead is the benefit you receive from engaging in your behavior.

For instance, someone who tends to misrepresent the truth might do so for the benefit of feeling important or getting their way. For whatever reasons, despite their belief that dishonesty is wrong, their operational beliefs contain a value that seeks the gratification that comes from their behavior. You can ask this question of yourself regarding gossip, sexual addiction, despondency, mistrust, or anything else that might be in your operational beliefs.

DOES MY PATTERN FOR MAKING CHOICES ACTUALLY HELP ME?

This question goes beyond the gratification factor and into the longer-term consequences of your choices. Be particularly honest in this part of your assessment. Maybe fibbing or bragging gratifies you for a while, but does it help you with your relationships? Have you experienced adverse results from the behavior? Are others hurt? Do your choices hinder your worship of God? Is your confidence built up by your behavior, or have you become more insecure over time?

We do what we do to survive and pursue happiness. Shortcuts and indulgence can undermine true survival and happiness. God commands behavioral choices for a reason.

He isn't out to destroy happiness, but to show how to achieve it. Remember, happiness is not the same as gratification.

HOW HAS MY BEHAVIOR SATISFIED ME IN THE PAST?

It helps to evaluate your behavior in light of how it has affected you in the past. If you can trace your behavior back to when you began to adopt it, that could help you analyze the reasons behind it. Just don't try to play amateur psychologist. Our guidance here is merely a set of questions to get you accustomed to strategic thinking regarding your own behavior and beliefs.

If you are able to evaluate past behavior that you continue to embrace now, you can move closer to understanding those hidden values in your mental software that motivate that behavior. Ask questions such as:

- How did it make me feel?
- What benefit did I think I received?
- Was the benefit long-term, or did I go back to my original frame of mind?
- What were the consequences of my behavior?
    - Did I get in trouble with my parents, teachers, or the law?
    - Did I struggle with guilt feelings?
    - Did my life improve as a result of this behavioral pattern?
    - What would God have thought of this behavior?
- What would have been a more effective substitution for my behavior?
    - How could I have acted differently?
    - What could the results have been if I took that alternate route?

- How might I have felt later that would have been better than the way I felt with the choices I did make?
- Would I have greater influence now as a result of the alternate behavior?
- Would my faith be stronger?
- Can I expect similar results now from behaving in a more effective way?

Again, we are not offering guidance in substitution of what a professional counselor might recommend. Instead, we offer a different way of thinking about your choices and behavior than what you may have now. It could be that having a *get to* mindset and evaluating your behavior in these terms might show you what some of your ineffective operational beliefs are and how you can change them into behavior that improves your life and relationships, including the one you have with God.

In the final chapter, we will distill the teachings of this book into some commitments you can make to get started on the path of strengthening your relationships.

AM I READY TO BUILD MY RELATIONSHIPS?

Learning, Empathy, Availability, and Intention

And if you offer yourself to the hungry
And satisfy the need of the afflicted,
Then your light will rise in darkness,
And your gloom will become like midday.
And the Lord will continually guide you,
And satisfy your desire in scorched places,
And give strength to your bones;
And you will be like a watered garden,
And like a spring of water whose waters do not fail.

(Isaiah 58:10–11)

Over a century before the nation of Judah fell to the Babylonian Empire, Isaiah prophesied it. He also offered encouragement that the destruction and captivity of the Jews would not be permanent, and that the mercy of God would release His people to go back to their land and rebuild the city of Jerusalem and its temple.

Through the prophet, God issued familiar promises conditional on the people's behavior. They were to obey Him, keep His Sabbaths, and practice justice, particularly mercy to the disadvantaged, just as they had received mercy from the Lord. The Scripture quoted above reflected that promise.

Isaiah's prophecies were directed to Judah, the nation of God's people. 95FIVE believes that it is important to be careful in how we transfer Israel–specific promises to individual Christians in the new covenant of Christ. However, God is the same and so are His expectations of behavior. Therefore, while old covenant Israel and new covenant Christians have different circumstances and a different orientation to God's laws (which were fulfilled in Jesus), both groups enjoy the same blessings respective to God's expectations of them.

In this, we can read what Isaiah said to the nation of Judah and find in his words the spirit in which we are to live. The lesson a modern Christian can take from these verses is that it is important to have a merciful and redemptive approach to others, particularly those who are afflicted or are in need. God blesses those who help them, and in fact had included provision for the poor as an important feature in His law for Israel.

The question that comes to our mind is that if we are to be kind and charitable to the needy and marginalized, most of whom we do not know personally, how much more should we show kindness and mercy to the people in our lives? Jesus promoted generosity to the poor (Mark 10:21) and He never brushed them off, but He acknowledged that poverty was an ongoing feature of civilization (Matthew 26:11). There will always be opportunities to minister to them, and we should.

However, there are not limitless opportunities to bless our relationships. If we do not build them according to the principles of Christ, our relationships may become stagnant, inactive, or damaged. Time is critical.

We will be blessed from our efforts to reach out to those having a hard time in society, but we need to make sure that our zeal for missions and ministry should not be at the expense of ministry to our relationships. There are poor people on the streets, but do you have family members or coworkers who are emotionally afflicted and burned out? Many around us are wounded and hurting physically, but what about fellow church members who live with invisible wounds, the emotional injuries that keep them in continual misery?

Chances are good you have many of those in your life, and you may not even realize it because you might be one of them. We have shared with you the reality of relational stress fractures and continued insult of pressure. If that is your state of being, it is no wonder you have difficulty recognizing the fractures and pain in others. Thankfully, healing of your fractures is available.

Hurting individuals exist in your life, however. They are important to you. Many of them you love deeply. Therefore, we feel we can apply the promise to Israel in their rebuilding efforts to those of us willing to do the work necessary to rebuild or strengthen our valuable relationships. We propose that "your light will rise in darkness" and you will be "like a spring of water whose waters do not fail" if you advocate for your loved ones and those who are in your orbit as much as you care about people in the mission field or those living in alleyways in your town or city.

What is your starting point? Begin with yourself, not because of selfishness but because you can't add as much value to others until you start on your own journey of effective strategy. If you have relational stress fractures, it is critical that you learn how to manage your pressure and stress responsively, rather than reactively. It will make a lot of difference in how you view the responsibilities and challenges of your life. Embracing a *get to* mindset will help you make this crucial shift.

Second, create a strategy to help you build margin in your life. You need financial margin and practical margin for your time management, goals, and expectations. These are fruits of wise pressure management. You also need relationship margin. As we have seen, pressure is compounded significantly in our connections to others, increasing the pain in both you and them.

Third, equip yourself to have more effective influence on people. We suggest the following four components to include in your approach:

1. Learning
2. Empathy
3. Availability
4. Intention

LEARNING

You have learned how our beliefs, perception, character, and pride are the factors that determine how influential we are in our relationships. Be a student of learning more about these parts of your thinking process so that you can continue to improve in your relationship ministry.

Don't let your ongoing self-assessment turn you inward and create in you a self-focused spirit.

Rather, regard this inner pursuit as a necessary discipline to make yourself more productive so you can continue to add quality into the lives of others.

We have also found that it is critical to be a student of other people. We don't suggest you do investigatory work to find out the secrets and personal affairs of those in your life. That would be inappropriate and unethical. However, we encourage you to learn about them as individuals. What do they love or hate? What encourages them the most? How are they emotionally blessed by what others do for them?

Learn what their interests and aspirations are. Pay close attention to how they best receive guidance without being defensive or discouraged. Learn the art of listening. What is the secret to that art? Asking questions. Learn to ask focused questions and be genuinely interested in their responses. You aren't collecting information to hold over them; that is manipulative and predatory. Instead, you are learning how best to add value to their lives.

Most people love talking about themselves, not because they are arrogant, but because they are sharing what they find important. Some of them will promote themselves with their personal narratives, and you will occasionally wade through self-focused talk. That's okay. It is a part of your ministry to them. With God's help, you can discover the gems in their soul from what they share with you.

You aren't out to diagnose them or assess their behavior. You have your own thoughts and behavior to worry about. Your role is to discover how best to advocate for them and help build them up emotionally and spiritually.

EMPATHY

Empathy is the ability to relate to someone else's feelings or point of view. You may not feel what they do at the moment, but you learn to see matters from their perspective. It is a wonderful human skill.

Why is it important? Because it puts you on their side. People need that if you are to gain influence with them. A couple of things to understand about empathy are:

- Empathy does not mean you know how someone else feels, but that you acknowledge why they feel the way they do, and you see the matter from their frame of reference as far as you are able.

- Being empathetic does not mean you agree with why someone feels the way they do or the behavior that comes from it. Being on someone's side does not always mean you are going to help them along in their present course of action. It means you will work for the best possible outcome for them and for others who might be affected.

When we are empathetic, we declare we want what is best for the other person. We are not there to judge or convict them, but to help them on the path to a wise course of action. People are not as likely to take your counsel to heart if you lack empathy for where they are. They need to know that you are on their side and want the best outcome for them.

A good example from Scripture is the story of the woman caught in adultery (John 8:1–11). Jesus came to teach in the temple courtyards on a morning during the feast of tabernacles. A big crowd gathered to hear Him. Suddenly some religious leaders brought to Him a woman they caught in the act of adultery. They reminded Him of the death sentence in the law of Moses for such activity.

Jesus stooped down and began writing something in the dust with His finger. They persisted in questioning Him until He stood up and said, "He who is without sin among you, let him be the first to throw a stone at her" (verse 7). Then He went back to writing in the dust.

As He did so, the accusers left the scene, leaving the woman by herself. Jesus stood up again and asked if there was anyone left to condemn her. She answered that there was no one to condemn her. He answered, "I do not condemn you, either. Go. From now on do not sin any longer" (verse 11).

This is a very popular story because it beautifully depicts the mercy and restoration of Christ. However, it is also a story of empathy. Jesus practiced the skill of empathy for this woman.

We aren't told His thoughts, and we don't need to be told that He disapproved of adultery. But where others with an agenda manipulated her life and potential fate to score a victory against their adversary, Jesus was willing to be on the guilty woman's side with a view of bringing her back to a path of righteousness.

He didn't approve of her sin, but certainly He understood the potential circumstances that brought her to the point of making the choices that she did. He knows the frailty of our emotions and the nature of pressure that drives us to do what we do. Jesus wasn't interested in her execution or in her continuing in her sin. He was interested in her restoration. In a powerful moment of accountability, He set her free, not just from her accusers but also from her emotional bondage. Empathy is perhaps the most influential skill to have.

AVAILABILITY

Availability is the best ability to have. It literally is your ability to avail yourself to others, that is, to be useful to them. Availability is your opportunity to strengthen your relationship and add value to the other person.

It might be safe to say that trust and availability are the greatest expressions of margin in a relationship. Through them you build credibility. The other person must grow to trust you, and that won't happen if you are not there for them.

What hinders your relationship–building availability to others?
- Self-focus
  - Distraction
  - Lack of strategy
- Reactiveness
  - Avoidance
  - Deflection
  - Blame
  - Resentment
  - Frustration

- Sense of obligation
  - I have to
  - I ought to
- Unaddressed relational stress fractures
- Ineffective operational beliefs
- Self-centered perception
- Pridefulness

We have discussed these in this book. The result of each of these is insufficient availability to others, which amounts to diminished influence. Provide a sense of presence in the lives of your people so they won't feel like they are an afterthought to you. Be available.

INTENTION

Finally, be intentional. Give your relationship strategy a sense of purpose and be aspirational in your approach to your relationships. Following are some resolutions we ask you to consider embracing as your own statement of intention, which will bring meaningful change in your life and in the lives of the other individuals you are connected to.

I WILL BE RELATIONAL.

This might sound obvious in light of the subject of this book, but if we are to be intentional in our relationships, we must first be intentional about avoiding a self-centered perspective of life and pursuing instead a life approach that places critical importance on the health of our relationships with others (chapter 3).

I WILL LEARN AND APPLY WISDOM IN MY RELATIONSHIPS.

The prime expression of wisdom, as we understand it, is strategy. Effective strategy consists of purpose, inspiration, accountability, and measurable results (chapters 2 and 8).

I WILL CHOOSE TO RESPOND TO MY PRESSURE RATHER THAN REACT TO IT.

Responding to pressure is more effective than reacting to it in an emotion–based way. Pressure–management strategy analyzes the pressure and your stress that comes from it. It asks questions. Reaction relies on an emotional state to struggle against painful feelings brought on by pressure and stress (chapters 4 and 5).

I WILL ADDRESS ANY EMOTIONAL DAMAGE THAT I HAVE, NOT ONLY FOR MY BENEFIT BUT FOR THAT OF OTHERS IN MY LIFE.

Relational stress fractures weaken our ability to manage pressure. They also compound stress in our relationships, making them less productive and healthy (chapters 6, 7, and 8).

I WILL MAKE THE PRACTICE OF CIVILITY A TOP PRIORITY IN HOW I MANAGE MY RELATIONSHIPS.

Civility is the beginning of influence, which is what we must have to build and strengthen our relationships. As long as we express hostility, we cannot build trust and credibility with others. Civility is the key to how we effectively relate to people (chapter 9).

I WILL EMBRACE BELIEFS BASED ON GODLY PRINCIPLES AND TRAIN MY PERCEPTION TO EXPRESS BEHAVIOR THAT IS INFLUENTIAL.

It is important to learn how to assess our belief structure and reject any values that stimulate ineffective behavior that damages our influence (chapter 10).

I WILL PURSUE EXCELLENT CHARACTER AND AVOID PRIDEFULNESS SO THAT OTHERS CAN TRUST ME.

Let your pride defend positive values while you learn behavior that builds positive character. Others will see you as someone who is trustworthy and credible (chapters 11 and 12).

I WILL BE ASPIRATIONAL IN HOW I MANAGE MY RELATIONSHIPS.

Learning, empathy, availability, and intention are the guidelines for a pursuit of healthy relationships. Be purposeful, show patience, model good character, and seek the best possible outcome for each situation.

Healthy relationships are the key to a satisfying life. Many people who want it all or have it all experience deep dissatisfaction because they don't have productive relationships to support them or give them a sense of true accomplishment. We can imagine how God must feel when many of His children sacrifice their relationships in the name of kingdom building. He would say to those people that to build His kingdom they need to build the relationships He gave them.

You aren't going to be one of those well–meaning individuals who miss the mark in their perception of serving Christ. Consider the above resolutions and prepare yourself to begin the most holy work you can do on this earth.

CONCLUSION:
BASED ON WHAT I HAVE LEARNED, SHOULD I CONSIDER A MORE EFFECTIVE STRATEGY?

*So then, be careful how you walk, not as unwise people but as wise,
making the most of your time, because the days are evil. Therefore
do not be foolish, but understand what the will of the Lord is.*
(Ephesians 5:15–17)

Imagine yourself on top of a mountain ridge, looking down at the wilderness you will travel through, just like Frank did on Mount St. Helens the day he almost got lost. In your case, the mountainside is your life, consisting of all your relationships. It is your future.

You have your compass and map. You have your pack equipped with supplies. God has given you what you need to be a powerhouse of support and credibility for those in your life. Whatever He has called you to do in His kingdom, it does and always will include the care of your relationships as your greatest area of service to Him.

Along with your map, compass, and pack is His kind admonition to "be careful how you walk," choosing wisdom and the stewardship of your time to make your life count. "The days are evil" means that hidden ore deposits along your path can distort the reading of your compass and lead you off course, even if just a little.

Most of your relationships will be fine, but there are plenty of opportunities for damage to creep into a few of them and render them less productive and purposeful than they could have been. Therefore, we must "not be foolish, but understand what the will of the Lord is." The ministry to your relationships is His will. It is your most important job, beginning with the one you have with Him.

Thankfully, it is rarely too late to turn matters around if you have a struggling relationship. Depending upon the damage already sustained, you may or may not restore it to what it might have been, but guess what? Christ redeemed all of that, too. As a service of stewardship to Him, you have the opportunity to change the way you think and react in powerful ways that can make a significant difference in your life and relationships. It's up to you to get started. Just ask if it makes sense for you to consider a more effective strategy.

When your journey here is finished, what your people will remember the most is how you affected them, the memories they shared with you, the kind of person you chose to be.

How you impacted their lives and the lives of others will be what they focus on. It is hard not to think that perhaps in heaven we will be judged and rewarded according to similar standards.

Ultimately, it takes faith and willingness to learn from the Lord and follow His example. You will mess up at times, but you can enjoy a life of continual improvement and joy. We believe you will do great.

WHERE TO GO FROM HERE

You have finished reading about some of the relationship skills necessary to manage pressure and conflict while building strong and productive character qualities and authentic influence in the lives of others. We showed you questions to ask yourself to assess where you are in reference to each of the concepts that involve effective relationships.

Now we have one last question: What will you do with what we shared with you about effective relationship influence?

This book is a launch for those willing to live authentically and powerfully in other people's lives, which is what God expects of us. The real journey begins, however, when you step out onto the path we show you in the 52-week program that elaborates on the relationship skills you learned about plus has more that go along with them. Besides what you read about in this book there are twenty-four more specific strategy and influence skills that can make a big difference in how you express Christ to others.

We believe we have put into your hands an effective roadmap for the coming year to help you stay in the Scripture, pray with focus and fellowship with other believers on a deeper level than just visiting with them at church each week. With the purchase of this program, you are getting:

- Information contained in our six books that is organized specially for this 52 weeks of structured learning that will give you a Bible-based journey toward more effective discipleship and influence with others.

- **Multiple ways to learn each week** - This includes model stories, reading texts, podcast recordings, Bible studies and questions for journaling, which we recommend.
- **Interactive training modules** to help you remember the relationship skills taught in God's word.
- **Access to our growing online community** - We are partnering with other believers who are like minded to provide ongoing content and insight into how we approach discipleship and relationships.
- **The opportunity to be an ambassador** to your church and Christian friends who might want to participate with you.
- **Other resources to help you grow and become more effective** - We will add more resources and tools in the months ahead.

This means an entire year's worth of material - all yours as part of purchasing this program. We recommend going to **95FIVE.com** as soon as possible to get started. As we said at the beginning, this book is part of a bigger picture. The bigger picture is what you can do with these relationship skills while living out your testimony. What difference will you make? A lot, if you approach your influence strategically.

Here is how you can begin your journey:

1. Begin the program soon. Don't lose momentum by putting it off. It's already yours, so dive in.
2. As God's Spirit begins to open your understanding of His principles regarding relationships, pray about taking them with you into your church life. If you don't have a church, we urge you to find one. We all need each other in these challenging times.

3.   Begin to consider how biblical relational skills can make your personal story more effective in Kingdom building activity.

How might you accomplish 2 and 3? This is where micro groups come in. We believe that the beauty of our program is that we won't interrupt the regular teaching of your church's educational program. 95FIVE can be used as a group study for sure. We are working on material for that setting. However, it doesn't have to be.

What can happen is that regardless of what you are studying at church, our program can be something you work through personally. What will make the experience more powerful for you is if you find one to three other people in your church willing to go through the program with you. Now you have a micro group.

Your purpose will not be forming a clique or secret group; we don't support that. Rather, we are asking you to partner with some others who realize how important it is to improve their efforts in building effective relationships. We base the purpose of micro groups on three things:

1.   Affinity
2.   Advocacy
3.   Association

By affinity we mean learning with like-minded individuals. You don't all have to love the same hobbies or share any demographic categories. However, we all have the tendency to share a general perspective with certain individuals in our church. We feel that these are ones you can best learn with.

What we don't mean by affinity is that you form a micro group with someone just because they are your best friend, or are in church leadership, or are of the same age, for example. These can qualify but can also take away from your experience if they are not on a similar level of seriousness or ability as you in regard to these principles. Have wisdom in your choice of micro group partners.

Advocacy is the second basis for our idea of micro groups. You may have a different pace in digesting the material as the others but what you are doing in this partnership is saying to them, "I stand with you in this effort. I am a fellow traveler." We leave it up to the members of each group to determine what level of accountability they express regularly. We recommend some degree of accountability, but above all else you are submitting yourself to be an advocate for the other individuals.

Finally, we view association as an important part of micro groups. We don't mean your association with the other members of your micro group but with who you aspire to influence with the skills you learn. The natural and organic product of discipleship is Christlike influence in other people. This is where your advocacy of the other micro group members can really be critical. You help them in their efforts to influence their people just as they help you.

Strategic micro groups are
New Testament discipleship in action.

The early church met in homes, in public spaces, and often in the early hours before work, learning Scripture, praying together, and worshiping God the best they knew how. These small groups and micro groups became the engine of church growth as the community of believers spread farther out into the world.

Why can't we return to that today? 95FIVE believes we can, and should. Not only that, but how much more effective can we be with our modern technology? Let's not squander the opportunity.

Go to **95FIVE.com** and learn more about us, our program, and the SKILLS micro groups we talked about here. We believe effective micro groups consist of Spirituality, Knowledge, Influence, Learning, Liberty and Strategy (SKILLS). Those are the principles that guide us and we are convinced that they should define the aims and character of effective micro groups.

Catch your vision, strengthen your relationships, and be a person who pleases God in everything you do! You can find us at:

- Website - 95FIVE.com
- Instagram - @95Five.Official
- Facebook - @95FiveBookOfficial
- YouTube - @95Five

ABOUT THE AUTHORS

BRENT MAXWELL

Brent Maxwell grew up in the Northwest, where he came to love the mountains, deserts, and farmlands of his home state. He attended Oklahoma Baptist University and soon after entered into his pastoral ministry, which would last for thirty years. During his ministry in Portland, Oregon, he received further education at Golden Gate Baptist Theological

Seminary, Northwest Campus, in Vancouver, Washington. It was there that he increased his love for and determination to understand and teach the powerful doctrines of Scripture.

While living and pastoring in Louisiana, Brent reconnected with his friend, Frank, and together they developed *95FIVE*. His observations in both the faith–based community and in the secular workplace have provided rich insights into human behavior in relationships, but no more so than what he has experienced in his own life journey. He continues to communicate biblical wisdom in his teaching and writing, seeking to be more effective in serving the body of Christ.

FRANKLIN SMITH

Franklin Smith is a father of two girls who has spent a lifetime asking questions about how things are done, why they're done that way, and why we are here on Earth. These questions have led to a diverse life as he has searched for answers to what his role is and what it means to be a good human being.

This journey brought him face to face with the realities of his own character, behavior, and ability to manage pressure and stress. Unsatisfied with the results of the choices he made and how they directly impacted people who counted on and believed in him, he began to search for a sustainable solution.

He pursued the answer over a five–year period with the help of his friend Brent Maxwell. Together, they developed *95FIVE* as a resource for those who have experienced the continual insult of pressure in their personal lives, businesses, and relationships. Using the Bible as the primary resource to discern what God has to say about character, pressure, influence, civility, and relationships, Franklin and Brent identified key principles that are not just good for people but pleasing to God.

The process of exploring the weaknesses in his character has strengthened Frank's desire to please God with how he manages his life, his choices, and relationships as he continues to pursue restoration through accountability for what he can control.

A lifelong entrepreneur, Franklin has experienced the highs and lows of managing people and businesses over thirty years of business ownership and consulting. He continues to grow through his writing, music, and passion for entrepreneurship as he applies the principles on which *95FIVE* is founded.

www.ingramcontent.com/pod-product-compliance
Lightning Source LLC
Chambersburg PA
CBHW031512120626
46545CB00005B/1851